THE WAR AT WORK

A TALE OF NAVIGATING THE UNWRITTEN RULES OF THE HIERARCHY IN A HALF CHANGED WORLD.

Seth Mattison & Joshua Medcalf

ISBN: 0692827579
ISBN 13: 9780692827574

This book is dedicated to the courageous and bold leaders faithfully committed to the process of reinventing and retooling what leadership, influence, impact, and execution will look like in this new digitally charged and hyper-connected world. We hope this story serves as an inspiring road map of where we've been and where we're going as we move through this dramatic period of change and transformation. Together we'll write the future.

Love,
Seth Mattison & Joshua Medcalf

Last Door on the Left

One-thirty a.m. on a Sunday night brings a special kind of darkness to an office building, and the headquarters of Axis Medical Group was no exception. The Executive Suite seemed quieter even than the floors beneath it. Then… *click. Beep.* A keycard swiped in the reader, and the glass-and-aluminum doors swished open.

A man entered, wearing a rumpled three-thousand-dollar suit clearly cut for a fuller version of himself. He carried a bag from Home Depot under one arm and a long, bulky cardboard package under the other. It looked as heavy as it probably felt.

The man's name was Brian Kelly, and he was handsome enough for a guy just on the wrong side of his mid-forties. The lines around his eyes belied years of well-burnt midnight oil, but the dark circles underneath them were newer. Those came from a war, recently-fought, one he planned on ending tonight. Because there was something else alive in his face: *resolve.* The focus of man who'd been recently awakened.

He crossed the waiting area, finally stopping at the last door on the left. The package hit the carpet with a dull thud, as he set down the bag and quietly removed his suit jacket. From the bag, he dug out a dust mask, snapped it around his mouth. Safety glasses next, then a pair of work gloves. And finally, the box. Staples popped as he ripped it open and lifted out a single tool…

A ten-pound sledgehammer.

Brand new, hickory-handled, with a head of drop-forged iron that tapered to a blunt wedge. Brian balanced its weight in his hands. It *was* heavy. Heavy enough to get the job done. He turned to face the door, and froze. Centered at eye-level, a brushed-steel nameplate stared back at him: "Brian Kelly, Seniro Vice President, Orthopedic Group."

A simple title, it contained two things: authority, and identity. *His* identity, a badge of honor forged over decades. But right now it felt like a coffin he'd spent his entire career building around himself. For a long moment, he just stared at it.

Now or never, Kelly. This is it.

His grip tightened and he rocked back, letting the hammer gather momentum. Then, with the whipsaw power of a discus thrower, he swung — WHACK! The iron landed, cratering the door. Bits of fiberboard popped through the cracks like snowflakes.

First blood.

A force unleashed, Brian swung again and again. WHACK! WHACK! The metal frame bent and jutted at unnatural angles, peeling away big chunks of drywall. The hinges separated, bent, and finally, the door collapsed with a dull crash.

The walls were next. One strike after another, the hammer turned sheetrock to dust, twisting and churning and bursting through metal and fiber and wood. Like water eroding stone, Brian erased the walls he'd worked his entire life to sit behind.

With each swing, he chuckled. He remembered reading about an Egyptian king named Akhenaten who, in defiance of the religious order of his day, ordered every idol of every god but his own smashed to pieces, and every temple cleansed of the images once held sacred by the old establishment. *Guess I'm not the first one to do this.*

Finally he slowed, pausing. The walls gaped back at him, a swiss-cheese mosaic of dust and punctured drywall. Dawn glowed outside; in two hours, the office would be buzzing with life. But not right now. Now it was just Brian and his hammer, alone in the silence and debris. He bent down, wiping drywall dust from the brushed steel of his nameplate, staring at the letters: "Brian Kelly, SVP Orthopedic Group."

And slowly... Brian Kelly, likely no longer SVP of the Orthopedic Group, began to smile, sensing for the first time in a long time, he had the power to create a different story about his future.

Pack Your Bags

"What the hell were you thinking?!" Brian watched his CEO angrily pin-ball back and forth behind his massive desk. Hank Stephens wasn't given to emotion, but this was clearly enough to push him over the edge. "How can I not have you escorted out of here? You destroyed company property! HR and Legal are going to lose it!" He registered Brian's calm with concern. "Are you okay? Do we need to get you help?"

"Hank, I'm fine. This was dramatic, yes, but it's what I thought was necessary. Total autonomy, right? That's what we agreed on."

"I didn't know 'total autonomy' meant taking a sledgehammer to your own office! Why would you do something like that?" Hank rubbed his temples. "Look, here's the move: you're taking a leave of absence. I don't want to see you for a week."

Brian's eyes widened. "What about the deadline you just gave us?! Eight weeks was asking for a miracle already, and now you want to cut it even closer? You know what's riding on this! If we don't hit the numbers you gave us—"

"You're axed. *All of you.*" Hank shrugged at Brian's surprise. "You're a great leader, Brian. And frankly, your track record is the only reason I'm not firing you right now. But your actions have consequences. What did you think was going to happen?"

Those words rang in Brian's head as he walked out. He'd expected pushback, but nothing like this. If he didn't deliver, now it wasn't just him who would suffer: it was his entire team. The certainty he'd felt just hours before eroded into a mass of anxiety as he paced next to his car, waiting for the phone to pick up.

"Brian? I got your messages. Did you really just destroy your own office?" The woman's voice on the other end sounded both shocked and half-amused.

"Yeah, it didn't exactly go as planned. Now my whole team is on the chopping block." The woman listened patiently as Brian explained the situation, pausing after he finished. He waited, unsure. "Caroline? Still there?"

"I am."

"So? What do I do now?"

He could almost hear her smiling. "Now you go all in, Brian. Pack your bags."

"You know I can't do that, I need to spend my time with Heidi and the kids—"

"You need this more, trust me Brian. Heidi will understand. Now, I'm sending you a first-class ticket to North Carolina. A driver will pick you up when you land, and I'll meet you at the destination."

"What destination?"

"Call it a trade secret. I'll see you soon."

The line went dead, leaving Brian reeling. He'd gotten used to an element of the unexpected over the course of his friendship with Caroline, but flying across the country at a moment's notice was a whole new level. *Where would he meet her? Why?*

Seat 2A

Three hours later, Brian collapsed into his seat, exhausted. Despite the chaos, Caroline was right: Heidi was surprisingly supportive of him leaving. She seemed to know that whatever was going on, it meant Brian was trying to become a better man and leader. When he told her what he needed, she just nodded. "You're my husband and I fully support you. Caroline already called. Something has to change and I think this experience is what you've desperately needed. Go." And with that he was out the door.

He sipped a martini, settling in, when his seatmate arrived. "Walton, Russ Walton," followed by the obligatory first-class handshake. Russ was ten years Brian's senior, with the genteel polish and easy drawl of a Southern businessman. "So, you're headed to my fair state on business?"

"The opposite, actually. I'm on a leave of absence."

Undeterred, the man kept pushing. "What happened?"

Brian sighed, this wasn't exactly what he wanted to talk about right now. In fact, he almost didn't believe it had really happened. "Well, I took a sledgehammer to my office. It didn't go over well."

A beat of stunned silence, before the Southerner burst out laughing. "I've heard some strange tales in my day, but never one like that! What were you fixing to change by doing that?"

"Oh, it's a long story."

"And it's a long flight. I'm all ears, my friend."

A War at Work

"Look, I didn't just snap and go crazy out of nowhere. What I did was actually the end result of a long progression that began about two years ago, after I had a breakdown."

"The part with the sledgehammer *wasn't* the breakdown?"

Brian chuckled, "No, believe it or not that was as clear-headed as I've ever been. The breakdown was just a lot of things adding up at once. Everything I'd built my identity on had eroded; everything I'd put my trust in was gone. I was so stressed and burnt out I actually ended up in the hospital. Fortunately, a very good friend helped me find my way back. But it took a lot of rebuilding, and a lot of hard lessons about how the world was, how it's changing, and what that means for me as a leader."

"Your friend sounds pretty remarkable."

"She is. She not only helped save my job, she might have saved my life."

"Well, you know now I have to ask: what did she teach you?"

Brian chuckled. "I guess we have time for a few of the basics. The first thing she taught me is that whether we realize it or not, the world we're living in is a world at war. That war pervades many layers of society and culture, but where it's most pronounced is in the workplace."

Russ cocked his head, curious. "A war at work, huh?"

"Honestly, it's a war that's been going on since the beginning of time, but it's being considerably amplified right now: the battle between **hierarchies** and **networks**."

"Hierarchies and networks? What do you mean?"

"Well, let's start with the world of the **Hierarchy**. You and I know it well, because all those years we spent coming up the ranks at our prospective companies, we were learning its rules. Everything we were taught was filtered through it, and everything we did to move up reflected it." Sliding a cocktail napkin out onto his tray, Brian began drawing on it. "If we had an image that represented this view of the world, I think it would be this…" Brian held it up, revealing the unmistakable branch-like structure of –

"An org chart?" Russ squinted, recognizing it instantly.

Brian nodded, "Exactly. But this image represents so much more than just that. It's literally a worldview – and it's been so baked into our DNA that in many cases we don't even realize it's there. But make no mistake, it is. It's in our government institutions, our religious institutions, and our university systems... even our families. All the authority cascades from the top down. 'What Dad says, goes', right?" Russ nodded, catching on. "So somewhere along the way, we learned this unique set of rules that we all agreed to play by in order not only to survive this world but to get ahead in it: I call them the **Unwritten Rules of the Hierarchy**."

Russ grinned, "I think I might know a few! 'Always make your boss look good,' that's one. Oh, and 'never question authority.'"

Brian grinned, "See? That's what I mean by 'unwritten.' We all know them, even if they've never been put down on paper anywhere. If you think about it, there's a laundry list of them that the generation of leaders we came of age with can rattle off."

"But those unwritten rules weren't all bad were they?" Russ fired back.

Nodding Brian leaned in, "Of course not and the hierarchy itself is not inherently bad. I mean it fueled the greatest era of progress and production the world had ever seen through the 20th Century. Incredible efficiency and scale, distribution of authority and responsibility, remarkable progress, it just played out in a world and a marketplace that operated and moved at a very different pace then what were witnessing today."

"Speaking of today, if the Hierarchy is where we came from, what's emerging now?"

Brian flipped the napkin over and kept sketching. "Technology is reshaping and distributing power in new ways. We've all seen it play out all around us, from the Arab Spring to Uber and Airbnb. We're entering an era that will be known as the age of the networks. All around us, thanks to the digitization of everything, everywhere we look in our lives we are now entangled in networks. Networks of information, education, entertainment, connections, etc. and with them come remarkable change and progress but they can also create chaos, confusion, and disruption."

Russ sat back in chair and shook his head. "Wow. We really are entering an era of networks. I mean I totally see now but I guess I hadn't stopped to think about it's impact like this before."

Brain let out a sigh, "Neither had I. In fact, neither have most people. Despite some experts recognizing the network's impact on marketplaces, most are unaware of the impact it's having inside our organizations. In particular as the next generations of talent shows up. You know the ones that leaders and organizations so often struggle to connect with."

Russ acknowledged he was a part of that group struggling.

"You see Russ, for everyone born after roughly 1980, they were essentially birthed into this new world and as a result they act almost as a catalyst for change. They're the canary in the coal so to speak. It's not that they created this networked world or that they're the only ones that can see it. In fact, many of the behaviors and new attitudes that have emerged from this group born of network are being and will continue to be embraced by all generations. We're all more digitally connected and empowered then ever before. The youth simply give us early clues as to what will become universally adapted principles for approaching work and life."

Brian held up the napkin, revealing a web-like configuration of lines and points between them. "Where we've seen the world like a hierarchy, they see a **Network**: an interconnected web of people, resources, ideas, and information. They see what is, in essence, a physical manifestation of the virtual world of the web. It's a world without walls, where information is free and instantly accessible to everyone and participation and access to the game is open to anyone. In this world, the rigid levels of the Hierarchy not only seem foreign but often antiquated, and in many cases completely impractical."

Russ nodded, "I could see that."

"The flattening of the family org chart has also influenced them."

Russ smiled, "What do you mean?"

Brian nodded, "Starting around 1980 Russ the family org chart gotten flattened and I'll give you an example. Let's say you're at a family event, with your kids and grandkids, and the TV isn't working. Who do you ask for help?"

"Caydence, my oldest granddaughter. She's only 14, but there's nothing she can't fix."

"There you go! Caydence and millions of others her age have grown up as the CTO's, or chief technology officers, of their families. Because of that, they've learned an entirely different way of interacting with their elders. Families have never been so dependent on their youngest members to navigate life. These kids have grown up in a world where they are routinely asked to teach the adults in their lives how to use the most influential tools in human history! As a result, it's reshaped their views and relationships with authority figures in their lives. Often times they view these individuals as peers now."

Russ just shook his head. "Makes sense. But that way of looking at the world, doesn't it just lead to total chaos? Without someone at the top calling the shots, without rules and order, how does society not start to break down? Companies can't function, much less institutions like the government or military!"

"That's exactly what I thought in the beginning too Russ. It's easy to go there when it's the only world we've known. But here's the thing: it's not about whether the Network is better or worse than the Hierarchy, it's purely about what will serve us best in this new world of work. As more and more of the world becomes networked, more and more aspects of our organizaitons will need to be also in order to survive. Does that make sense?"

Russ took a sip of his water and nodded. "Feels a little overwhelming."

Brian smiled. "I get it Russ. I felt the same way. What helped me was understanding that just like the Hierarchy, the Network has some foundational truths of its own and unwritten rules that emerge from these new truths. These new rules often clash in direct opposition to the Unwritten Rules of the Hierarchy, leading to the whiplash that everyone seems to have experienced at some point in the past few years. At least I know I have."

"What are some examples of new unwritten rules?"

Sitting up in his chair, Brian smiled. "I'll give you three quick new truths and a couple of unwritten rules of the network to chew on."

"The first foundational truth is what I call ***Unprecedented Access.*** Essentially the network has vastly increased the volume of information that everyone has access to, raising people's expectations for truth, transparency, and openness. New unwritten rules coming out of this are things like information should be accessible, open, and free and when it comes to even the must virtuous authority figures, trust but verify."

"The second foundation truth of the network is ***Exponential Reach***. It's the idea that anyone can contribute and participate. The barriers to entry have never been lower. That's why you see 15-year-olds starting companies and getting funding for ideas. They can push an idea out in to the world that you and I would have never been able to at that age, and as a result they expect to contribute and participate when we perhaps think they haven't earned it yet."

"Third: ***Hyper Immediacy.*** It's an instantaneous word where individuals and brands can go from virtually unknown to worldwide recognition in less than 24 hours. That fact alone exposes the inefficiencies of the hierarchy, a world where speed and disruption are feared, and the next iteration is not only not embraced, but often discouraged."

Russ nodded, putting the pieces together. "Sure, I read about things like that all the time in *Fast Company*. But here's my problem with it: we don't live in that world just yet. Getting my company to sign off on a new product, that process still takes a year."

Brian just smiled, "That's because you've just hit on the big secret no one seems to talk about: <u>that we live in a half-changed world</u>."

"Half-changed?"

"Absolutely. Most companies aren't equipped to operate without some level of hierarchy in place. A plane will always need a pilot, right?

"At least today it does!"

"My point exactly. Today we still need pilots but as we continue to advance its possible to imagine a day where machines, not pilots do all of the flying. The same goes for the hierarchy. While the networked world is emerging, the structures of the Hierarchy, and more importantly its deeply-embedded culture, still exist in our world today. And so, those two worldviews do battle with each other, each and every day, in every single organization, and in every single workplace in the world."

Russ smiled, amazed. "The war at work."

"That's it, my friend. We're living in a half-changed world. And the solution to moving forward isn't to just write off the Hierarchy as a whole, or cling to the Hierarchy and avoid the Network. Instead, I think the organizations, businesses, and leaders who succeed in the next decade are going to be those who can find the sweet spot between these two worlds, and lead effectively while straddling the gaps."

Russ whistled, "How'd you learn all this stuff?"

"The hard way," Brian grinned. "It took a lot of work to 'get it,' and what I outlined is just the tip of the iceberg. There's so much more to—"

"*—ladies and gentlemen, please return to your seats...*" The captain's voice crackled over the speakers, interrupting.

As Russ buckled in, he shot Brian a grin. "We'll have to finish this conversation another time. But to be honest, I feel like I've got enough to chew on for the next year, just from sitting here listening to you! Many thanks!"

"I'm happy it helped you!" Brian nodded. "And I hope it can continue to help, beyond just you, into your circle. I know that's exactly what happened for me!"

"I'm sure it will," smiled Russ. He raised his plastic cup. "Cheers to that."

"Cheers, indeed."

The Abbey

Brian's curiosity grew as his Uber driver turned onto a long drive, passing under curtains of moss, hanging from the arching branches of live oaks. While excited, Brian also felt a bit apprehensive. Over the past eighteen months he had learned to trust Caroline and her sometimes unusual coaching methods but this was a whole new level. Shifting in the backseat of his black Town Car, he let out a deep sigh as they pulled up to a cluster of white buildings.

"Brian!" A beaming woman stood waiting for him. Dressed in simple clothing, she radiated a sense of peace and grounded strength in every word and gesture. She greeted Brian with the warm hug of a lifelong friend, "Welcome to Mepkin Abbey."

"Trade secret, huh? Where have you taken me and what are we doing here, Caroline?"

"We're here for total immersion training. I've taught you all I can for the past eighteen months, and you've made incredible progress toward becoming the transformational leader required to navigate the worlds of the hierarchy and the network. But Brian, some things cannot just be taught. They must be *lived.* And if you want to truly experience the breakthrough that comes from an authentic shift in your heart posture, there's no better place to do it than right here." She gestured around them as they walked toward the Abbey. Monks in long robes walked the grounds, some on their way to prayers, others to their work. "I hope you're ready, Bri. Over the next six days, we're going to go deeper than you ever thought possible."

Brian nodded with a mixed of both curiosity and hint of suspicion. Caroline had often described her time at the Abbey as a turning point in her own transformation, but Brian had always felt a little uneasy about the idea of monks, robes, and monasteries, never thinking he'd actually visit the Abbey.

"I love you Caroline but if you think I'm gonna be wearing a robe and chanting by the end of this week you're crazy!"

Caroline let out a laugh. "Let's get one thing cleared up buddy. This is not about converting you or frankly even about religion at all. There are remarkable, timeless lessons to be learned here simply by paying attention to how these individuals live their lives and operate their businesses."

Brian's eyes widened, businesses?!"

Caroline shot back, "Yes, business! I fill you in more as the week progresses but people travel all over the world to study the business insights from these monks. No one is here to convert you I can promise you that. It's not a cult Brian but if you're willing to be present to the moment, I'm certain the next few days will have a tremendous impact on you as a leader."

Brian let a sigh of relief. "Alright Caroline. I'm with you. What's first?"

Caroline grinned. She threw him a pair of gardening gloves. "Follow me."

Feel and Real

"When you said 'let's get started' I didn't think you meant weeding!"

Brian laughed, wiping sweat from his face. He and Caroline bent over a flowerbed, pulling weeds by hand. Dirt caked their hands, as she laughed. "Well, someone has to do it!" She threw their pile of weeds into a nearby wheelbarrow, which was being pushed by a tall, gregarious man in jeans and a T-shirt.

"Are these ready to go?" He smiled, introducing himself as Augie. He and Caroline had become friends at the Abbey years ago, and he seemed to know a lot about Brian already, addressing him with a heartfelt directness. "So Brian, Caroline tells me you've been having a problem navigating the difference between 'feel' and 'real.'"

"I'm not sure what you mean?"

"Let me ask you this. Do you golf?" Brian nodded, as Augie continued. "Have you ever taken a golf lesson where they show you your swing on video, and then they show you a pro's swing video side by side to yours?"

"Yes I have, but it wasn't pretty!" Brian answered with a chuckle.

"So what usually happens in those lessons is that after they show you the other swing, they give you something to do to make your swing look closer to the pro's swing. And then you swing again. And Brian, so many people think their swing is going to look so different and better simply because it *felt* different. Then imagine their face when they turn around and their second swing looks *exactly the same* as the first one!"

"Are you sure you weren't at my last lesson, because that's exactly how it went!"

Augie let out a booming laugh. "Well, there's a good reason for what you experienced. That's the gap between 'feel' and 'real.' It's the exact same thing in business and life. I know that you and Caroline have been working for a long time on navigating the shift between the Hierarchy and the Network and from being a transactional leader, to becoming a transformational one. The only way to do that, is to close the gap."

Caroline jumped in, "That gap is why you can still experience setbacks after years of training. You might feel like you've been doing everything you can to become a transformational leader instead of a transactional one, but until you experience a true change of heart, strategy and technique will only get you so far."

"You'd never guess it, but this Abbey runs several of the most effective businesses on the planet," Augie continued. "And thus, many people come here to learn and copy the business strategies and techniques of the monks. But they never get the same results, because they haven't had an authentic heart posture shift. Just like the golf lesson, they *feel* like they have made big changes, but if they saw themselves on video they would realize those changes are minuscule at best, and nonexistent at worst. Most people are just checking boxes, but checking boxes will never allow a person or organization to fulfill their true potential."

Brian nodded, grasping it. "So that's what this week is really about."

"Yes, Brian." Caroline nodded. "It's about closing the gap between 'feel' and 'real.' The monks here call it *caritas*, and it means living from the heart. Living with authenticity."

Augie grinned at Brian, "Look, I know this is going to be a challenging week. But I promise that if you open your heart and approach this experience like a child full of curiosity, you will walk out of here freed up to become the very best version of yourself. But before we dig into all of that, how about you tell me how you and Caroline got here in the first place?"

Brian nodded, glancing to Caroline with a smile. Then, he began his story…

1994: First Day of the Rest of Your Life

The dot-matrix glow of an alarm clock shifted as the numbers clicked from 5:59 to 6:00, and the radio crackled to life. Brian's hand slapped it to silence, but he'd been awake for an hour already. A bundle of ragged nerves were busy twisting his stomach, heart, and mind together into a single clenched-fist knot of pulsing anxiety.

Today was the day. His first day at Axis Medical Group. His first 'real job.'

He showered, shaved, and pulled on his suit. It was the second suit he'd ever owned. Not much need for one growing up in the blue-collar Kelly family. In fact, his father always had a union worker's distrust of suits; to him, a suit meant "the Man." So when he looked Brian up and down with suspicion instead of pride the first time he saw him in it, Brian tried not to take it personally.

Ray Kelly was a loving man in his own way, not that it was ever obvious. But he'd always worked to provide a good life for his family, and he never once complained. Just kept showing up for year after year of double shifts on the mill floor. Brian remembered nights he came home so bone-tired that he didn't even bother squeezing out of his steel-toed boots. Instead, he just collapsed in his La-Z-Boy, sawdust still clinging to his Levi's.

All so I could get here, thought Brian as he knotted his tie. He was the first in the family to graduate college, and the first to land a job at a desk. He knew how lucky that made him. His base salary was already twice what his dad made in a year. He checked himself one last time in the mirror and couldn't help smiling.

This is it… the first day of the rest of my life.

Axis

"Here we go, Mr. Kelly. This is you."

The matronly HR rep stopped in front of an empty cubicle at the far edge of the Sales & Marketing cluster. Brian gave her a warm smile, "Thanks."

"Don't forget to report for orientation at ten in the conference room. Oh, and welcome to Axis!" She bustled away as Brian unpacked his briefcase next to the computer, realizing how bare his desk looked. *Not for long.* He knew he'd be drowning in stacks of work soon enough. As he settled in, a woman's voice floated over the cubicle wall –

"So, they stuck you out here on the frontier too?" Surprised, Brian looked up to find a willowy young woman smiling back him. She offered her hand, "Hi, I'm Kerry."

"Brian Kelly," he replied as they shook hands. "Is that short for Caroline?"

She nodded, "It is. Growing up, I was the girl who'd rather shoot hoops than play with Barbies, so Kerry fit better."

Brian nodded, realizing that he trusted her immediately. Kerry marched to the beat of her own drum, but not in a way that made enemies. She was smart, tough, and confident; someone you wanted on your team. He nodded to her cubicle, right next to his. "Marketing right? Why are you out here? I thought Marketing had their own floor."

She shook her head, holding up her orientation binder. "Sales and Marketing are basically one department. Lots of crossover. Didn't you read the org chart?"

Brian blinked. "The what?"

"The org chart! It's basically your map of the company. Here..." She flipped to a page mapped with a tree-like structure, a pyramid of names descending in an orderly grid. Her finger moved over each level, "CEO, Board of Directors, EVP's, SVP's, then the VP's, and Directors, and Managers, and then, all the way down here..." she stopped at the lowest level, "...you have Associates and Analysts. Us."

Brian smirked, "Speak for yourself. I'm an 'Account Executive.'"

Kerry rolled her eyes, "You're a *salesman.* Don't try to get fancy on me. Have you met Hackworthy yet?"

"No, I got assigned to his team after I was hired, so—"

"Brian Kelly?" Brian turned to find a smiling, well-manicured man a few years older than him. All five feet, six inches of him was spit-polished to a practiced sheen. "Neil Hackworthy, Sales Manager." He shook Brian's hand with impersonal vigor. "You two ready for orientation?"

Brian nodded agreeably, "Of course, lead the way!"

Welcome to the Jungle

As the tour group wound through floors of orderly cubicles, Brian couldn't help thinking: *this is a lot like school.* That kind of institutional order made sense to him. *Input X effort, reap Y result.* Being the last guy off the court had always served him well, and he hoped it would do the same here... especially when he saw where it might take him.

The Executive Suite was a different world, a world of polished marble, sleek leather chairs, frosted glass, and thick oak doors. The energy was calm. Unhurried. Powerful. This is where real change happened. As if to prove the point, a pair of VP's swept past them into the Executive Dining Room. The new hires caught a quick glimpse of long tables, linen napkins, and heard the clink of silverware on china as the Axis upper echelon shared war stories, office gossip, and chef-prepared meals.

Brian just stared. *I bet one of those surf-and-turfs costs a quarter of my paycheck.* But to his surprise, that didn't make him envious or angry. Instead, it <u>motivated</u> him. That could be him in there, eating lobster and steak and sharing war stories. Why not?

The tour finished in a first-floor conference room, where Neil ran the group through page after page of policies and procedures. Brian's eyes glazed as they flipped through corporate binders, until... *BANG!* he jerked up, startled, as the door flew open —

— and a salt-and-pepper-haired colossus of a man swept in, booming a loud, "Morning, troops!" The entire room shot up in their seats, immediately at attention. As Brian would quickly learn, this man tended to have this same effect wherever he went.

"I'm Ed Barkley, and I'm your boss. Welcome to the American Dream!" he boomed, pacing. "You're now a part of one of the fastest-growing companies in the world's greatest economy, and with a little elbow grease, you have the chance to make a life for yourself that your grandparents only dreamed of. How many of you are the first in your family to go to business school?" Brian felt a rush of pride, raising his hand along with Kerry and a few others. Ed nodded. "You're the ones I'd watch out for. Why? Because you're *hungry*. And that hunger gives you an edge." Ed stopped pacing. "But you're going to need it, because as dynamite as our product mix is, as good as our leads are, our competition will eat your lunch if they catch you slipping."

Heads nodded as Ed went on, "Make no mistake: whatever it is you want out of life, you can earn it here. But you have to be willing to sacrifice for it. Hustle your tails off. Sales, get ready to pound the phones and the pavement. Marketing, get your minds right, we need you to dig deep and put the time in to help us find the angles and close deals!" Ed gestured to Neil, "Now, you'll get all the details you need about policies and procedures from this guy. You'll hear about memos, and meetings, and about how things are done around here. You'll even hear about *why*."

He indicated a framed poster, denoting the Axis 'Mission Statement': *Healing the world through innovation, progress, and connection.* Ed gave the room a knowing grin, "At the end of the day, yes, we do sell things that help the world, and that's a nice thought to fall asleep to each night. But you know what's nicer? Falling asleep to it on nine-hundred-thread-count sheets in a master bedroom by the beach. That's what I call a good night's sleep." The room rippled with appreciative chuckles.

"But that's not something that just happens overnight. Because believe me, you are not here for policies, or procedures, or memos or meetings. You are here to do one thing, and one thing only: close sales. *Ink on the line,* that's all that matters. Welcome to the jungle, folks. You only get to eat what you kill." Brian nodded, the knot of nerves re-awakened in his chest, as Ed paused, every eye in the room glued to him.

Then he exited the room like he entered it: no outro, no goodbyes, no handshakes. Just a slammed door and ringing silence.

"Any questions?" Neil grinned, scanning their faces. Clearly he'd heard this enough times to appreciate the effect it had on new recruits. Brian looked around, realizing: they all wore the same look of awed, awakened energy. *No wonder this guy is in charge of Sales.*

Sink or Swim

"I actually remember going to sleep that night," Brian reminisced as he, Caroline, and Augie walked back toward the dining hall. "And before I drifted off, I just kept feeling the sheets, and thinking, 'Boy, I don't know what nine-hundred-thread-count feels like, but I do know this: as soon as I can afford it, I'm going to find out!'"

They laughed, Caroline chiming in, "I felt the same way, but about the parking spaces."

"The parking spaces?" Augie asked, curious.

Caroline nodded, "You know, Exec Parking. They all had their assigned, personalized spaces, but I had to walk ten minutes each way from the satellite lot across the street."

Augie chuckled, "Sounds like you were both entering the deep end at the same time."

Brian nodded, "This much was obvious from day one: we were in a different world. And it was time to sink or swim."

Fired

Brian's first week at Axis passed in a blur, and before he knew it, it was Friday.

The shouting started at five-thirty pm as the team started to pack up for the day. A ferocious burst of anger began to emanate from Barkley's office. BANG! The door burst open and Dan Berg, a longtime sales rep, charged out in a huff. "This is BS, and you know it! They were my clients!"

Mike Jacobs, several years his junior, wasn't far behind. "I'm sorry Dan but you weren't servicing them effectively. You left money on the table, don't blame me for your timidity!"

"It wasn't timidity Mike, it was friendship! Those people had been with us since the beginning; those relationships took years to build! "

Jacobs held up his hands, "They're your clients, Dan. Not your friends."

Ed followed them out of his office. "Berg, the decision's final, I'm sorry. We wish you the best." His meaty hand jutted forward, challenging Berg to resist. Finally Berg slumped, the fight going out of him. He pumped Ed's hand, mumbled something incoherent, and retreated to his cubicle, defeated.

"Come on, people. Show's over." Neil Hackworthy appeared and began waving everyone back to work. Brian couldn't help asking —

"What happened?"

"Sounds like Berg lost his edge. He ignored the directive and didn't raise rates on the bottom half of his client list for the last two quarters.

Jacobs figured it out, and pushed a few deals through that Berg should have handled. Easy choice for the big man." He nodded to Barkley's office, and made a slashing motion across his throat.

Brian blinked, alarmed. "But that seems so shady."

Neil grinned, "I wish I'd thought of it." He noticed Brian's shock, waved it off. "Look, it might be harsh, but it was also effective. Jacobs has a new office, Berg's packing his into a cardboard box, and Ed gets to eliminate a full salary and benefits from the bottom line, while one salesman now does the work of two. Everybody wins."

"Except for Berg."

"Kelly, there's only so many spots on the bus. Success is a zero-sum game. If someone's winning, someone else is losing. Dan's a good salesman and a really nice guy, but nice won't get you to the Boardroom."

Brian nodded, those words searing themselves into his mind, as Carter Bowles, one of the Marketing Managers, jostled past. He thumped Neil on the shoulder with a grin. "Almost 'Corner time,' Hackworthy. See you there?"

Neil slapped his back, "You know it." He clocked Brian's curiosity, grinned. "Friday night tradition. Couple of us head to the Corner Club for scotch and cigars."

"Sounds like a blast. You got room for one more?"

Neil chuckled, "Not for you, rookie. Managers only. Perks of the title, you get it."

Brian flushed, burning with embarrassment. "Right, sorry."

"Plus, tonight you'll be busy doing something else: my homework." *Thump.* Neil dropped a thick folder on Brian's desk. "These are all the orders from every Sales Manager. Get 'em logged by Monday." He grinned, noticing Brian's crestfallen face. "Don't sweat it, Kelly. You gotta pay your dues. I had to do the same thing my first year here." Brian just watched as the Managers exited in a pack, laughing and back-slapping.

"Like rush week all over again, isn't it?" He turned to find Kerry, watching from her own cubicle. She held up a thick folder identical to Brian's. "You're not the only one. Carter wants thirty emerging market reports analyzed by Monday."

Brian chuckled, "Ouch, that's even worse than mine." But Kerry just shrugged it off, calm. "What's wrong? Why aren't you more angry about that?"

"Because, I'm not afraid to be here until the lights go off." Brian just looked at her, confused. "You gotta know how to grind, Brian. Did you play sports?

Brain fired back, "Of course. High school. Football, basketball and baseball."

"Then you get it. Talent only takes you so far." She smiled. "I had an amazing coach in college, he taught me something I'll never forget. See, I was the highest-recruited player on the team, but I'd coasted on talent my whole life. My fundamentals were terrible. So he benched me. He told me, 'Kerry, if you quit when everyone else quits, don't be surprised when you only get the results everyone else gets. You need to decide what kind of player you are: the kind who quits when practice is over, or the kind who keeps practicing until the lights go off.' So, I started staying late after every practice. It took two seasons of hustle, but by the time I got my shot as a junior, it paid off." She spoke with a quiet intensity. "Anyone with talent can merely be *good.* But no one, talent or not, can be *great* without hard work."

Kerry brightened, holding up her binder. "Plus, Carter thinks this is busywork, but he's wrong. It'll give me an edge in how we market to similar areas in the future." Brian nodded, impressed, as she scanned the now-empty office. "You hungry?"

"Yeah. I was thinking about ordering something in, if you—"

She waved him off. "Come on. I've got a better idea."

"YOU'RE ON."

Twenty minutes later, they sat in the cozy corner booth of a restaurant that seemed to be half-sports bar, half-sit-down steakhouse. A few neon signs cast their electric glow over the place, while the one over the bar announced the restaurant's name: *Bentley's*. Brian took it in skeptically, "This was your 'better idea'?"

"Hey, it's better than cold takeout in the cubicle." Kerry smiled as the waitress arrived with their drinks; "Martini for the gentleman, and a Long Island for the lady."

As she whisked off, Brian raised his drink, "Here's to making it through week one."

"Cheers!" Kerry sipped. "And you can say that again. Did you see Berg and Jacobs this afternoon? That was crazy. I don't want to end up like those guys."

"Hey, I wouldn't mind Jacobs' client list. Or his new office. Or his Mercedes."

Kerry agreed, "Same here. But is any of that worth it if you end up becoming a jerk?"

"Of course not," Brian shrugged, playing devil's advocate. "It might have been coldblooded by Jacobs, but if Berg were a better salesman and put his company first, this wouldn't have happened. It's just business." A beat of silence as Kerry nodded, admitting — what Brian said sounded right. He continued, "But if it makes you feel any better, I don't think you have to worry about that. At least not while I'm around."

She sighed, "Thanks. Same here. But that doesn't mean I won't get promoted first."

Brian laughed, "You think you can?"

"I think I *will.* Give me three years."

"Fine, I'll do it in two and a half."

Kerry laughed, but he knew he'd just kicked her competitive side into high gear. Sure enough, she ordered two more drinks, turning back to Brian, "Let's make this interesting. I'll bet you one drink per week from now until our first promotion that I'll get it first. Whoever gets promoted first picks up the tab."

"Shouldn't it be the other way around?"

"No way. What's the point of a raise if you don't buy your friends drinks with it?"

Brian laughed as their drinks arrived. He raised his glass, meeting Kerry's eyes. Enjoying the challenge. "Fine: you're on."

She clinked her glass against his, and took a sip. Then, "Here's one caveat. I think we can make this work for both of us, regardless of who gets promoted first. I've been getting the sense that there's some guidelines to operating at Axis that aren't exactly in the manual. So if we want to get ahead, we'll need to know them."

"You mean like a playbook?"

"Exactly!" Her eyes lit up, as she grabbed a napkin and a pen. "Stuff like what we just saw. Berg gets fired and Jacobs gets a promotion. We grind for the weekend and the higher-ups celebrate with cigars and single malt. Reserved parking spaces and special dining rooms for executives. I'm sure there's a whole list of them, and we if we don't learn them, we're gonna end up stepping on a landmine."

Brian smiled, catching on. "So to avoid the landmines, we keep our eyes and ears open and capture as many as we can. We rally back here every week and share what we learn. And to be honest, I think we have to if we want a chance at surviving here."

"It'll give us an edge, that's for sure." Her eyes flashed, "But beyond that, may the best man win."

Brian just smiled back. "Oh, don't worry. I will."

The Recipe for Success

The weeks began to pass in a rapid haze of late nights and early mornings as Brian fell into a steady rhythm at Axis. Despite promising to do so several weeks in a row, he quickly realized he hadn't seen his parents in months.

So the next weekend found him arriving at their home, just in time for Sunday dinner. His mother greeted him with her hug-and-fuss routine, while Ray offered the usual gruff handshake. As they sat down to the same Sunday evening pot roast Brian had loved since he was a kid, conversation turned to his new job. While his mother clearly enjoyed hearing about this foreign world of wining and dining clients, chasing leads, and landing contracts, Ray just acknowledged it all with a wry nod.

"Sounds busy. You sure they're not working you too hard at that desk?"

There was an edge to Ray's voice that Brian had heard many times before. This wasn't a question about his well-being; it was a question about his performance. Ray was a "results guy." To him, the measure of a man was his ability to take the hill and grind it out every single day. Knowing this, Brian had his answer ready, "Well, we're growing pretty fast, so most people put in sixty hour weeks."

"And what about you? What kind of weeks do you put in?"

Brian shrugged, "Punched out at one last night, so that makes it eighty this week."

It wasn't quite a smile. But for a second, Ray's face relaxed, even creased at the edges a bit. Brian couldn't believe it: he'd seen that expression only a handful of times before, while playing sports in high school. Pride in the old man's face. He realized later, that simple display was more than enough to motivate him for years after. But for now, he swallowed his shout of victory, and kept the conversation going.

After dinner, he joined Ray on the porch as the old man lit his usual Pall Mall. Brian broke the silence. "How's the mill?"

Ray grunted, "Coming up on thirty-two years next week. Just gotta make it three more, then your mother and I, we're heading south."

Brian grinned, "Nine before nine, right?"

"That's the dream." His years on the mill floor would earn Ray an RV and six months a year in a retirement park in Arizona. He'd made no secret about his plans once he got there: nine holes of golf before nine AM, every single day of the week. "I'm telling you boy, it goes fast. My first day at the mill was in '63, seems like yesterday." Ray exhaled, smoke rising around him. "Didn't know my ass from my elbow."

Brian smiled, "And now you're basically running the place."

Ray chuckled, more reflective than usual. "Want to know how I did it?"

Brian grinned, "Of course!"

"Well, my third month on the job, my Lot Manager got fired. I thought, 'Hey, this is my lucky day, I'll go show my supervisor how I have all these ideas about how we could do things better around here, and maybe he'll promote me. Boy, my ears were smoking when I walked out of that office. And this old-timer on my line, he lit into me. I'll never forget what he said." Ray chuckled, "He said, 'Kelly, you're a smart kid, but don't get too smart for your own good. Want to know the recipe for success around here? *Put your head down, keep your mouth shut, work your tail off, and don't try to skip any steps. Do that long enough, good things will happen.*' That's exactly what I did, and I ended up climbing the ladder right on time. You want to move up at that office of yours, you need to do the exact same thing."

On the drive home, Brian pondered his father's words. *'Keep your head down, your mouth shut, don't skip any steps.'* Thinking about life at Axis, it seemed to make sense. He repeated it over and over, intent on putting it to good use over the years ahead.

"NEVER. AGAIN."

Brian walked the length of the Boardroom, taking his place at the far end of the conference table. It felt a mile long. It was his first multi-divisional meeting, and he was excited to present his progress in landing a few key clients in new markets. The buzz quieted as Ed entered, followed by two other VP's and a phalanx of Managers.

Ed launched the meeting, and as each team presented their reports, the knot of tension at the center of Brian's chest grew tighter. Finally, it was his turn. He swallowed his nerves and calmly outlined their sales growth in a few key areas. As he did, Burke Rawlings, VP of Supply Chain, interrupted him. "So let me get this straight, if they hit their production numbers, we're looking at real competition from both Arthrex and RTI in the spinal market next year?"

Ed jumped in, "No, Arthrex is solely sports medicine."

Brian blinked, confused. *Wait a minute, that's not right.* Without thinking twice, he interrupted, correcting Ed: "Actually, you're thinking of Alphatec. They're still only joint, trauma, and sports. Arthrex has been announcing their move into spinal for the last six months, and—"

He trailed off, noticing: the air in the room had just died. Every eye, most of them wide, was locked on him. He froze, a flash of panic hitting his gut as Ed leveled a glare his way that stopped the blood in his veins. He quickly looked away, flushing, as Ed, undeterred, kept right on speaking as if nothing had happened.

As the meeting wore on, Brian's dread grew. How much trouble was he in? Was he about to be called into Ed's office? As the finally room cleared, Brian quietly circled the knot of higher-ups near the doors. But just as he thought he'd made it out safely...

"Hey, hotshot." He turned to find Ed, eyes fixed on Brian. Brian's mouth went dry as Ed growled simply but directly, "Never again. Got it?"

Brian swallowed his fear. "Yes, sir." And that was it. Ed moved on, as Brian wandered back toward his cubicle in a grateful half-daze.

"Kelly!" Neil flagged him down, a look of half-concern, half-amusement on his face. "What the hell's wrong with you!? You just publicly challenged Barkley. I've seen better salesmen than you kicked off a team or reassigned for less!"

"I'm sorry, it just came out. But honestly, I didn't think it was frowned upon. Are we just supposed to sit there and say nothing when the higher ups are misinformed or just flat-out wrong about something in a meeting like that?!"

"You can disagree, sure, just not publicly! Plus, that's what a chain of command is for. If you see something like that, you run it up the proper channel. Your job in that moment is to find a way to make your boss look good and toe the line." Neil chuckled, "You're a lucky man to catch Barkley on a good day. Next time you might not be so lucky."

As Neil walked off, Brian sank into his chair, breathing a sigh of pure relief. He knew Neil was right, he'd gotten lucky this time. No public outburst of wrath, no barrage of insults, no promise of future judgment hanging over his head: just two words. *Never. Again.* But they had the desired effect: the lesson had been irrevocably branded into his mind, and he knew he'd never forget it.

"ALWAYS MAKE YOUR BOSS LOOK GOOD."

Brian was determined to make his mark at Axis, and to make it faster than anyone else. Month after month, he was first on the floor in the morning, and last out at night. He and Kerry quickly distinguished themselves as "the hardest workers in the room," each benefitting from the help the other freely offered. Sales and Marketing went hand in hand, and their shared insight continually put them ahead strategically.

But where Brian succeeded with perseverance, Kerry's secret weapon seemed, ironically, to be her softer side. She'd always had a way with people; coming from Kerry, "How are you?" never sounded like a line. And coupled with her sharp mind for analyzing market data, that innate emotional intelligence earned her plenty of success. Their corner-booth powwows at Bentley's quickly became a necessary ritual as they blew off steam, shared war stories, and captured aha's from the past work week.

And if Brian were honest, they needed all the help they could get. Despite their hard work paying off with clients, getting it noticed by Barkley was something else entirely. Most weeks, he spent ten minutes with the 'worker bees,'and was inaccessible the rest of the time.

One weary Thursday night found Brian and Kerry in their booth, working on their "playbook" and comparing thoughts on emerging markets for the Imaging division at Axis. The quarterly meeting was next week, and they knew this was a rare chance to get an idea in front of the higher-ups. They were determined to make the most of it.

That's when lightning struck; Kerry had a moment of inspiration that resulted in one of "those" ideas, the kind that both she and Brian were instantly electrified by. It could reposition a product they'd been having trouble with in the marketplace for years, removing a thorn in the side of management and resulting in job and funding growth to their departments in the long run.

Brian shook his head in sheer jealousy. "I can't believe I didn't think of that! You're going to look like a genius when you pitch that on Monday."

Kerry's smile wavered as a thought struck her. "Actually... what if I don't pitch it? What if I feed it to Barkley?"

"Are you crazy? He'll take the credit! This is your meal ticket, you can't give it away!"

Kerry shook her head, impassioned. "You have to see the bigger picture. This could benefit all of us, it makes our whole department look good. We get more visibility, maybe even the funding we need to expand. A rising tide lifts all boats, right?"

"Sure, but it doesn't get you promoted. And it's your idea! Don't you want the credit?"

"I do, but I'm not sure taking it will help me get ahead. One of the rules we need to add to our playbook is something I've been noticing: '*Always make your boss look good.*' Who doesn't love a worker who makes them look like a genius?"

"I don't know, I'm not sold. I also see a lot of people keeping their best ideas close to the vest. It gives them an edge!"

"But not when it comes to your boss, Brian. Trust me." Brian couldn't change her mind. And on Monday, when he pulled Kerry aside to check in, he was too late. "I already pitched it to him on the way in. He loved it!"

Brian deflated. He knew Kerry was brilliant, but to him this seemed like career suicide. "When he takes all the credit for it, don't say I didn't warn you."

Kerry just smiled, confident. "Just wait and see. It'll pay off."

The next week, a hush lay over the Sales & Marketing division as the quarterly meeting let out. Ten gray-haired, blue-suited men strode in: the

Board of Directors flanked by various executives. The CEO of Axis stepped forward —

"Ladies and gentlemen, today is a big day for this division. You've got some growing to do. That's right, you're expanding!"

Cheers broke out as Kerry flushed, elated. Brian couldn't help half-hugging her, smiling wide. "We've solved a longstanding problem, all while increasing our market presence in three new sectors. And it's all thanks to someone I want to recognize right now—"

Brian's smile widened, watching Kerry's eyes glow with anticipation, until...

"—your fearless leader, Ed Barkley. Come out here, Ed!" A gut-punch of disbelief ripped through Brian, as Kerry wavered on her feet. Barkley smiled wide, accepting the thunderous applause as the CEO went on, "You're lucky to have such an ingenious man in charge here, and you can all pick up a thing or two from his example..."

Brian squeezed Kerry's hand in silent support. She was crushed, but her calm never wavered. She shrugged, "Well, you did warn me," Later, as the party wound down...

"Kerry!" Kerry turned to find Ed. "Step into my office, would you?" Curious, Brian watched as she and Ed entered his office and closed the door. Was she in trouble? Was she being praised? Even after she walked out, it was impossible to tell. Brian pulled her aside, anxious. "What happened? Is he going to promote you?"

"Not yet. He just told me I was an incredible team player, thanked me for putting the company first, and told me to keep up the good work."

"That's it? Wow. I'm sorry, that's so terrible..." Bet or not, he knew he'd be ecstatic for Kerry if (and when) she were promoted, even if it happened to her before him.

She shrugged and waved him off with a knowing smile. "It's okay. Just wait for that rising tide to come in someday. You'll see what I mean."

The Tide Rises

They didn't have long to wait.

Just three months later, Kerry was promoted to Manager of Marketing Analytics, a new division begun in large part thanks to her work analyzing the reams of data that her old Manager plopped on her desk every Friday. True to her word, she followed through on her bet with Brian, paying his 'one drink per week' out of her first new paycheck.

And while her promotion scratched Brian's competitive itch, he truly couldn't be happier for her. The day she moved into her new office, he gave her her first desktop gift: a set of tiny cast-iron boxing gloves, "Because you're always punching up..."

Kerry glowed, encouraging. "Don't worry, you're next." Sure enough, six weeks later Brian was tapped as the Sales Manager for the new Orthopedic division. Kerry rewarded him in kind, with a small bronze pair of basketball sneakers, "Because you're always the last one off the court."

Life was good, and they both knew it. As Brian and Kerry continued their ascent at Axis, time brought changes beyond just the office. On a market research project, Kerry met a handsome young surgeon named Jack Hilden. A week later, Brian began dating Heidi Jung, a supply rep at a wholesaler Axis had taken over. The couples became fast friends, creating memories together as Brian and Kerry began enjoying the fruits of their labor; nights out at five-star restaurants, vacations to Mexico and the Caribbean, new BMW's for both of them, and a new designer wardrobe for Kerry.

They worked hard during the week, and played hard on the weekends. Because as their personal lives grew more complex, so did their careers: authority, it turned out, came with a whole new set of responsibilities.

"INSUBORDINATION CAN'T BE TOLERATED!"

"I can't take it any more. I think I'm going to fire Kevin Walker." Over their usual drink at Bentley's, Kerry vented her frustration after a long week. "He's one of my sharpest guys, but I just can't take any more of his pushback. He questions every decision I make. He has no loyalty to the team, no respect for the party line."

"Are you sure you're not overreacting a bit?"

"What do you mean? He's clearly being insubordinate."

Brian shrugged, "Look, you're the only female Manager in Marketing, you've got it a lot tougher than anyone else. But are you sure you're not just being overly sensitive?"

"Yes!" Her passion rose. "This guy is a nonstop thorn in my side! The past few weeks we've been trying to push these new market dynamics reports up the mountain on a deadline. Of course, this means a lot of tweaking as we go, which is to be expected. But honestly, if I hear him disrespect my feedback one more time–"

"Maybe he's just trying to be helpful and improve what he thinks needs fixing?"

"Well he's got a funny way of showing it. Today we were presenting to a client, and he interrupts and contradicts me, right there in the room!"

Brian nodded, admitting, "That's pretty bad."

"Especially in front of the client, that's Meeting Etiquette 101! It's disrespectful to both the client and the company. I'm not saying I'm not open to his perspective, but there's a time and a place for it." Kerry continued, "I'm just saying that at some point he needs to realize that he's the employee, and I'm the boss: for our team to function correctly, insubordination can't be tolerated." Brian couldn't help but chuckle, as Kerry's eyes flashed. "What's so funny?!"

"Nothing, sorry," he answered. "It just sounds like something that would've gone up on the wall in the locker room back in high school. Or Ed Barkley's office!"

"As it should. What would've happened if you had mouthed off to your Coach, or refused to do drills the way he'd said? You'd pay for it, right?"

Brian nodded, the memories still with him. "Until I collapsed."

"I don't know, maybe Kevin never played sports, because he seems to have missed that memo. He has no respect for the title, or the structure that's in place. And if he keeps going like this, it just makes me look bad to the higher-ups."

Brian sympathized, "Like you don't have control over your people."

"Exactly." She drained her drink. "And if that happens, it's bad for everybody. It makes the whole department look bad. So in the end, he's really only hurting himself."

Brian nodded as he signed the check. "Well, do what you have to do. That's the job. Like Ed says—" Kerry joined in, "—'*it's lonely at the top, but somebody's gotta do it.*'"

They chuckled at that 'old-timer' bit of wisdom as they parted ways, but Brian had begun to appreciate its truth lately. The perks of management did come with a few downsides, and he'd found himself missing the camaraderie that one could enjoy as a lower-level salesman. People treated you differently as a 'boss.' Co-workers he'd considered close were now more guarded, keeping him at arm's-length.

He shook it off as he climbed into his BMW and fired it up. He'd fought hard to get where he was, and he wasn't looking back. *Business is the jungle*, he thought, remembering Ed's speech on that first day. *If you don't adapt, you don't survive.*

And Brian wanted to do more than just survive the jungle: he wanted to thrive in it.

The True Cost

"And thrive you did, I imagine."

Brian and Augie worked alone in the pre-dawn damp of the Abbey gardens. Caroline was off in her meditation practice, and would join them later. Augie had listened to Brian's story for hours, and showed no signs of tiring.

Brian continued, filled with conflicted nostalgia. "We thrived more than I ever thought possible. I got everything I ever wanted, but I had no idea of the true cost."

"The 'true cost'? What do you mean?"

"I mean that all that time, little did we know that we were instilling a whole worldview deep into our hardwiring, one that valued money over relationships, that reduced success in life to a number in your IRA and a title on your office door."

"It wasn't just you, Brian, it was our whole nation. An entire culture built around buying things we didn't need, with money we didn't have, to impress people we didn't like. I'm just as guilty of that as anyone else."

Brian shook the dew off another clump of spinach. "I guess we were just doing what we could with what we had. In some ways, I can't blame us."

"And you shouldn't," Augie smiled. "But as we all know, there's a bottom line to living that way.

Brian nodded, sober. "And we crashed right into it..."

2008: Everything You ever Wanted

No alarm clock this time. The pre-dawn darkness of Brian's bedroom was pierced instead by something far more effective to a parent: the cries of a two-year-old. He threw off the duvet and stumbled across the hall to his daughter Ava's room. Holding her, he descended the stairs, slipping into the kitchen.

Even six months after moving in, he still couldn't believe he and Heidi had been able to build their dream house. Five bedrooms, four baths, a sprawling basement complete with a home theater and an indoor basketball court in the sub-basement. The kitchen had Italian marble countertops, hand-blown glass for the overhead lighting, and Brian's favorite, Brazilian cherry floors. It meant a quadrupled mortgage payment, but he could more than afford that right now. After taking his Sales team in Orthopedics to an all-time earnings record two years in a row, he'd finally been promoted to VP last year.

He'd had one night to enjoy it, before the reality of the new job kicked in hard and fast. Because while the medical equipment and services industry had experienced some clear growth over the past decade, Axis had skyrocketed, nearly tripling in size. They were one of the big guys now, thanks to Ed Barkley's rise to CEO. His take-no-prisoners approach meant one thing for Brian: more work than ever. There was barely a moment of each day he wasn't putting out fires or playing catch-up. Some days, it felt like his Blackberry never stopped buzzing.

Today was no exception: he'd barely finished dressing Ava when the first few emails came in. One of his sales teams had dropped the ball on a crucial account, and the client was thinking of leaving. *Be there in an hour,* typed Brian.

When he woke Heidi up, she wasn't happy. They'd agreed to take Ava to the doctor together later that morning. "Can't you just stop there first, *then* go into the office?"

Brian gave her a *what do you expect me to do?* shrug. "They need me now."

"Why?"

"Because I'm the boss."

"Doesn't that mean you're in charge of your own schedule?"

Brian shook his head, "Not if there's a problem. If there's a problem, it means that I'm the one who has to solve it."

She sighed, not the first time they'd had this exchange, "But there's always a problem."

On the drive into the office, her words rolled around his head. What else was he supposed to do? This was his job. It wasn't his fault that he had become vital to the operations of the division. Plus, it made him feel like he was earning his keep. His division needed a leader who covered all his bases and was available to solve problems when required. It wasn't his fault that they often needed him at odd hours of the day and night.

As he pulled into the Executive Parking lot at Axis, Brian shook his head. *She'll understand someday. Earning your best life doesn't come cheap.*

He had no way of knowing now just how right he was.

Blindsided

"I'm confused. Didn't we already have a meeting on this last week?" Brian and Kerry walked through the bustling, now-merged Sales & Marketing corridor.

As VP's, they still worked closely together, doing their best to move the massive machinery of Axis forward. But these days, that was harder than ever. More divisions, more territories, and more layers between them and the front lines meant a slower flow of information and a higher risk of being blindsided by shifts in the marketplace. Implementing change, experimenting with new ideas, and responding quickly had become a thing of the past. The new daily reality was meetings to talk about meetings.

As they approached the Boardroom, Brian shrugged off Kerry's question. "I honestly don't know, Ed didn't say. I'm sure it's just routine." But the moment they entered, they knew this was anything but. Any time this many department heads – everyone from Managers to VPs to SVPs – were in the same room, it wasn't a good thing.

They took their seats, as Barkley began. "Look team, there's no other way to put this. We anticipated another big year, but given how the economy's affecting healthcare, that's not going to happen. In fact... we're looking at some significant losses. We overshot our landing on expansion in a few key areas. Peter's passing out the financials, so you'll see for yourselves, but the headline is, they aren't good."

Brian flipped through the folder, realizing that 'the financials aren't good' was a substantial understatement. They were brutal. A hand shot up across the table. "If this is right, we're bottoming out on <u>three</u> over-leveraged divisions? How is that possible?"

Barkley nodded, "Frankly, each of them faced significant disruption from newcomers to the market that we didn't anticipate. Customer erosion happened too quickly to receive the resources and attention needed to address those particular issues. Now, this doesn't mean we're not secure. We are, which is why we're all here having this conversation. But it does mean we'll have to tighten our belts in some of these departments. "

Every mind raced at once. *Is it me? Is my department? Are the hundreds of people and millions of dollars in resources that I represent at this table, on the chopping block?*

Barkley pushed his reading glasses up, emotionless. "Now, obviously the first to go are those three divisions. We don't have the overhead to keep them running."

Kerry raised her hand. "What does that mean for the Marketing Analytics group? Half of my current staff is wrapped up there—"

Ed shrugged. "Then effective tomorrow, half your staff is no longer essential."

Kerry blanched, whitening. "But that's hundreds of people..."

"This is the only way to keep your division viable. It's going to be a leaner ship, sure, but this means you can make it through the storm. It's that, or shipwreck."

Brian could feel her hurt and frustration building, and for good reason. Of all the executives at Axis, Kerry was well-known for taking the time to know her employees, often celebrating their birthdays, weddings, or the birth of their children. She shook her head, her anger thinly veiled. "This isn't their fault, though. It's ours. We didn't see this coming, or worse we did and we were too fearful to face it. Our expansion was based on our own growth models, which were much too aggressive—"

Ed cut her off, "It's not up for discussion." He addressed the rest of the room, "Now, we don't want this getting out there too fast. We need to control the story. So for now, keep it to your top people. No news is good news, that kind of thing..."

His voice droned on, as Brian looked over at Kerry. She was stronger than almost anyone he knew, but this might be too much for even her to take.

"WHAT DO I DO NOW?"

That night found Brian and Kerry back where they'd shared this hour of the workday so many times before: their old corner booth at Bentley's. There were cracks in the leather now, but the same neon glow lit the walls, and that corner booth still felt like home.

For once, neither wanted to talk. While Brian's department would escape the cutbacks unscathed, the reality of what Kerry faced tomorrow weighed on both of them. Eventually, she spoke. "What do I tell them?"

Brian shrugged. "The facts. They'll understand."

"I know they'll understand, on paper. But Brian... what do I *tell* them? How do I tell these people that trusted me with their careers, who follow me every single day of the week, that we just led them all off a cliff? This is not their fault, it's *ours.* They shouldn't have to pay for our mistakes."

"What else could we have done? You heard Ed, its bad timing. We expanded a little too far too fast. We rode the same wave as everyone else."

"Yeah and now three hundred people are losing their jobs. People I'm responsible for."

"You're not, though. You're responsible for doing your job, and that means following Ed's orders. You keep your head down and you take the hill." Kerry just pushed a few ice cubes around her glass with a straw. Brian went on, "Facts of life: he's the boss, he makes the rules. That's how life works. Think about playing sports growing up. Who made the rules?"

"Coach."

"Right. Same with our families. Was it a democracy? Hell no. The family agenda wasn't up for discussion, it was up to your Dad. He *said*, and everyone *did*."

"And how did that turn out for you and Ray?"

Brian felt a reflexive flush hit his face. Knowing she'd hit a nerve, Kerry backed off. "Look, all I'm saying is that just because it's how we were raised, doesn't mean we have to do the same. I mean you hated never having a say. Are you raising Ava how you were raised?"

He admitted, "No."

"And I'm not raising Jackson and Parker that way either. I'm giving them space to be themselves. We talk to each other. It's a discussion, not a monologue. Even if we still make the final decision, we do it together. I know when we were growing up, it was all about, 'children should be seen and not heard,' and somehow that made it into the workplace, too. I don't think it's a good thing." She waved her hand, weariness kicking in. "I guess I'm just wondering how to do this honestly tomorrow, when none of my people have done anything to deserve this."

"They're not your people, Kerry. They're your employees." Brian shrugged, feeling as helpless as she did. "You know as well as I do; this is just the way things are, and they always have been."

"But do they have to be anymore?" The words hung there, electric.

After a moment, Brian just shrugged, gave her hand an encouraging squeeze. "You'll get through it tomorrow, I know you will." But as much as Kerry wanted to believe him, her silence told him otherwise.

THE EXODUS

The next day seemed to last forever. Employees trickled from their cubicles in a blank-faced exodus, like trauma victims trying to grasp what had just happened. When the building finally emptied at night, Brian walked down to Kerry's office. Inside, he found her at her desk as usual. But for once, her professional calm was gone. She looked hollowed, exhausted, like something elemental had changed in her.

He hesitated. "How are you?"

"How do you think?"

Brian nodded, unsure what to make of the emotion in her voice. That's when he saw it: a cardboard box, sitting at her feet, filled with a few books, framed pictures, and… that tiny set of cast-iron boxing gloves. "Wait a minute. Are you packing your things…?"

He looked up, confused. But there was no confusion in Kerry's response. Just resolve. "I resigned fifteen minutes ago. I can't do this anymore, Brian. Today was the last straw."

Brian reeled, "But it's over! You should be drinking champagne because you still have a job, not packing up your desk because you don't want one!"

"It's not that I don't want a job. I just don't want this one."

"Why not?! I get this was painful, but we're not the only ones facing this. Do you realize how many companies are doing this exact same thing right now? Plus, you're on track for SVP in the next couple years, a year faster than we thought–"

"Honestly, I didn't say anything last night, but for the life of me I just can't understand how little this is affecting you! How you can be so self-centered that today doesn't bother you is just beyond me. It's not the Brian that I know."

Brian exploded with indignation, "What?! You don't think this is bothering me?!"

"You have a funny way of showing it, talking about promotions and breaking out the champagne, all while the blood's still fresh on every floor of this building."

"Kerry! Of course it affects me, but this is the real world, and sometimes in the real world you have to make hard decisions. That's the cost of doing business. That's the cost of driving the 5 series. That's the cost of sending Jackson and Parker to private school. That's the cost of playing the game at this level. You know that!"

"Oh, I do. I'm just not sure I want to play it anymore. I'm not sleeping. I haven't worked out in months. I can't remember the last time I wasn't distracted at dinner with emails and text messages. Life's just too short. There's a better way to live, there has to be."

Brian fired back with fresh cynicism. "Great. Well, when you find this mystical 'better way,' be sure to let me know."

She shook her head, weary. "Why are you being like this?!"

"Why are *you?!* You think I'm selfish because I want to keep my job? I just want to feed my family! In case you haven't noticed, we're in the middle of a recession, and not all of us have it as easy as you do. I can't just check the diversity box on a job application."

Kerry blinked, unbelieving. "*Excuse me?* What the hell did you just say?!"

Brian froze, trying to backtrack, "I just meant there's a lot less competition for an ambitious executive who's also a woman of color—"

Brian's voice trailed off as the shock, anger, and pain on Kerry's face became clear. "Are you serious right now?! Fifteen years I've known you, and *now* you're gonna start using the race card with me? And you have the gall to tell me how *lucky* I am to be an African American female?"

Brian opened his mouth to apologize, but she cut him off. "Just stop talking." Silence fell, as Kerry stood, stony. "Goodbye, Brian."

"Kerry, please. I didn't mean it like that, you know I didn't. I'm sorry."

"You've made yourself clear. I wish you all the best." For a moment, she softened. "I just hope the Brian Kelly I've known for so long doesn't get lost in his race to the top."

Stunned, Brian walked out of the office, simultaneously burning with shame at what he'd said, but also confused by Kerry's choice to leave Axis and leave him. It just seemed so *rash,* so out of character for her after everything they believed in, everything they worked for. But her words rattled him. "*There's a better way to live, there has to be...*" Was she right? Was the cost of 'doing business as usual' unforgivably high?

Brian was starting to get the sense that something was changing in the world of work. A shift had occurred and try as he might to apply the old rules of success, the formula seemed to be evolving.

Intent on moving forward, Brian pushed the thoughts away. Tomorrow would be a new day. Tomorrow, the world would move on.

From There to Here

"And indeed the world did move on," Caroline added. "For both of us." She and Brian sat with Augie, overlooking the peaceful waters of the Cooper River, which wound past the Abbey.

Brian stirred, "Speaking of which, I still have some questions about that. You never told me the specifics of what you did right after you left Axis."

She smiled, "Winston Churchill once said, 'Those destined for greatness must first walk alone in the desert.' And while greatness is a lifelong process, I've definitely walked alone through the desert. That's what I did after Axis."

"That still doesn't answer my question!" Brian shook his head, but before he could say anything else, Augie jumped in —

"And neither of you are answering *my* question! You can't just leave me hanging like this. Obviously you worked past how things ended that day. How did that happen?"

The old friends exchanged glances. Brian just nodded, "Well, a lot happened from there to here. But for me, it had to get a lot worse before it got better..."

2014: What's Going On?

The roar of voices grew louder in the darkness, crackling with tension. Thousands of masked faces blurred together, moving forward in unison, until — *Thunk! Whoomp!* Riot gas spewed through the crowd, as the police moved in. Camera flashes painted the stark image of a single masked young man standing against them, raising a black umbrella in each hand.

A newscaster's measure voice cut in —"*the fifth day of what is being called the 'Umbrella Revolution,' Hong Kong fell into chaos today...*"

Alone in his office, Brian swiped out of the video on his iPad, disturbed. What was going on? The world seemed to be going crazy. And for once, the answer couldn't be found in the office around him. It was the corner office now, even bigger than before. But it somehow felt smaller than a cubicle. Because while the past few years had brought even more success, they'd also brought more challenges.

Healthcare, like so many industries, had been upended. Once the secret no one wanted to talk about, disruption was now front-page news. Change was the new normal. Communication, customers, even information itself had evolved in ways that sometimes seemed unrecognizable. Every landmark Brian had charted on his way up the ladder seemed to have either moved or eroded and given way to something completely different.

His life was a nonstop treadmill of late nights, early mornings, and well-meaning vacations where family time eroded as quickly as the emergencies popped up back at the office. Despite another title bump, pay bump, and increased responsibility, Brian felt more and more like his life was just the constant management of a single ongoing crisis.

A knock on the door interrupted his lunch. "They're ready, Mr. Kelly." Brian heaved himself out of his leather chair, feeling each of the thirty pounds he'd packed on. Stress had its price, and working ten-hour days didn't make it any easier.

"We don't have time to sugarcoat this, the numbers don't paint a pretty picture." Hank Stephens, Axis's current CEO, was a small man, but the energy in his voice took over the room. "Our Net Promoter score continues to slide, and nearly every single one of our top-performing verticals has seen an exodus of top talent. All except for yours, Kelly. Good work."

His eyes held on Brian, who fought cold sweat. Right now, this was the only thing keeping him viable: despite a slide in client retention and market share, he'd still managed to keep his team together and focused. For now.

"But let's talk about your other numbers. You're getting crushed in most markets, and this is the third quarter in a row you've been off projections. What's going on?"

As Brian fought through his answer, he knew that despite the external forces he was fighting in the marketplace, the internal ones at Axis were becoming just as tough. 'There are only so many seats on the bus' had never felt more true than it did right now, and the battle for 'seats' had never been more fierce. Not only was he competing against industry rivals for contracts, but the infighting within Axis had grown more toxic. However he was going to get out of the hole he was in, he'd have to do it alone.

As the meeting wrapped, Brian looked down at his watch, and instantly wished he hadn't. He was late by an hour already. *Again.*

A Better Life

"Honey... you can't keep doing this."

Heidi poured herself a glass of wine, glaring at Brian. After Brian missed his son Jameson's ballgame, they'd just finished putting their tired and cranky kids to bed. Feeling tired and cranky himself, Brian just fired back, "It's not like it's up to me! We're under the gun, and I can't help it if Hank keeps me overtime!"

"But you can set better boundaries, or at least manage the expectations of your kids who love you and want more time with their father in their lives."

Brian looked away, an eruption of self-vindicating frustration exploding in his voice. "What do you want me to do? I'm trying to give them the life I wish I would've had growing up! Sure, I miss some things because of work, but work is also the reason they have the best equipment and play in the best leagues and go to the best schools. Do you know what I would've done when I was a kid if I had all the stuff they have!? We got them iPads for Christmas last year! You know what I got for Christmas when I was their age? A baseball glove that probably cost four bucks!" He paused, noting her glazed eyes. This clearly wasn't the first time she'd heard this. "Look, I just want to make sure they have a better life than I did. I don't want them to have to fight for what I did."

"Don't worry, they don't. But they also shouldn't have to fight to get your time and your best energy, either."

Brian shrugged off her concern, "Look, I'd rather miss a few games and keep a roof over our heads than slack off and lose my division. I have to set the pace for my team. I set the expectations for performance and accountability. I have to be out front on these things and hold myself to a higher standard."

"Ok but can't you at least delegate more, hand some stuff off so it's not always on you?"

"To who? Half my team is twenty-five years old and working their first real job! I care about them and I want them to do well but they're not ready for a lot of what's on my plate. It's just not that simple."

"So train them. Give them the chance to step up. Delegating isn't bad leadership."

"I know that, but it inevitably ends up making more work for me in the long run. It's like my dad always said, 'you want something done right, do it yourself.'"

"And how did that work out for him?" Heidi's eyes flashed. "Brian, our kids have one childhood. One. I hope you don't wake up one day realizing you traded it in for iPads."

She spun on her heel and left the kitchen, as Brian shuffled off to his office, angry. *Why can't she get it?!* But as he poured a scotch, something wouldn't stop gnawing at him. He stared at a picture on his desk: teen-aged Brian, smiling ear-to-ear next to a stone-faced Ray. He felt a pang of regret shoot through him, and raised his glass before taking a drink. "Here's to you, old man."

On nights like tonight, he wondered how different he really was from Ray. The thought sobered him more than he liked to admit, and for good reason. After all his decades spent planning and working relentlessly toward his dream of 'nine before nine,' Ray never got to play a single hole. The week before his retirement party, he was diagnosed with advanced pancreatic cancer, and he died two months later. Brian still felt the emotional whiplash from it. He'd been across the country closing a new client when he got the call that Ray was gone, and the sense of incompletion that hit him that day had never left. His father's death was a loose end that would never be tied up, a sentence that ended in a question mark, instead of a period.

It gnawed at him now, that emptiness that refused to quit. So he did what he always did; poured another drink, pushed the thoughts from his mind, and got to work.

Captain's Chair

"All right troops, let's get down to business." The room snapped to attention as Brian entered. "First priority: where are we at with EpiMatix?" With all of the recent shake-ups in territories, Brian and his orthopedic team had started selling a portion of the Axis ophthalmology product line. EpiMatix was a highly anticipated new amniotic membrane product designed for eye care.

"R&D and marketing are both saying it's ready to go. I think we've got a great story to tell the marketplace. We just need to push it up the ladder for final sign off." Even at 27, Austin Rhodes was already Brian's top rep. A young entrepreneur, Austin had launched a small med device start-up at 18. While the device never took off, his industry experience at such an early age was truly remarkable. A born leader, he reminded Brian a lot of himself. And while careful never to show favoritism, Brian often invested extra time shepherding the young rep.

"Marketing put together a solid go-to-market strategy and the projections look strong." Austin's team smiled, as he turned to Brian, buoyed by their energy. "So, when do you think we could get this up to the sixth floor?"

Brian felt the expectations that hung on this. Still, all he offered was, "Soon enough."

Disquiet settled over the room as Austin exchanged looks with Zach Bryson and Amy Keller, two young all-stars he worked closely with. The elected speaker for the group, he replied, "Is there any particular reason for delaying it?"

"Yes. Because it's not ready."

"But it is ready! Why are we waiting?"

"Because I said so." Sensing the disquiet, Brian softened, "Look, you've all done a great job so far. But our positioning and strategy just isn't where it needs to be. Trust me." As he scanned the room, no one met his eyes but Austin. The tension broke as he looked away, but as the meeting moved on, Brian knew this wouldn't be the last of it.

Darkness found Brian still at his desk, racking his brain for a solution. To stay viable at Axis, they didn't need a home run: they needed a walk-off grand slam. And to stay on top, he needed to be the one who hit it. But despite the buzz, Brian knew EpiMatix wasn't a game changer. Without the right re-positioning, it would be lost in the shuffle.

A knock interrupted him, and Austin swept in. "Boss, I think I figured out our move." With clarity and concision, Austin laid out his strategy. Just like Brian, he'd picked up on the fact that selling EpiMatix in the ophthalmology vertical gave it a big whiff of 'same old, same old.' His solution?

"We cross it over to Ortho! I know no one's doing it, but I think that's a pro, not a con. We'd have the entire market to ourselves." Brian knew immediately that the idea was a stroke of genius. Research on using membrane products in joint and extremity procedures was already in the works, and he'd even spoken to doctors about the possibilities. He'd just never put it together… until now. Austin couldn't contain his excitement, "Look, the actual product wouldn't have to change much. We just pivot the positioning and the story, because —"

"—the use is almost identical," Brian finished the thought. "We may not even need to get FDA approval. Which means, we could have this ready before next quarter." Brian sat back, thoughtful, "I can see it. Let me think it over before we share with the team."

Austin floated off, dizzy with the thrill of what he obviously knew was a slam-dunk. But that was exactly the problem, and Brian knew it. Pitching an idea like this up the food chain needed to come from the top, not the middle.

Brian knew exactly what he had to do. And worse, he didn't think twice about doing it.

Old Dog, New Tricks

The next two weeks flew by as Brian pushed the team to finish everything in order to present the product at the quarterly meeting. The energy in the department had completely shifted, and it showed: they pushed through product repositioning, testing, QC, and legal in record time, with green lights all around.

And when the time finally came to pitch it in the room, Brian couldn't help but watch with pride as Hank leaned back with his rare look of close-lipped approval. The product was approved unanimously, and Hank took Brian aside as the meeting wrapped. "You really pulled this one out of thin air, Kelly. Whatever you need to get it moving, do it. You have my complete support."

He even insisted on swinging by the division to spread the good news. Amidst the cheers, he pulled Brian forward. "You're all lucky to have this guy at the helm," he laughed. "Turns out the old dog here really does have some new tricks. His vision to shift EpiMatix from ophthalmology to Ortho is going to be talked about for years to come. Now let's go make it happen."

As Hank swept out of the room, Brian noticed Austin and his team in tight-faced conversation amongst themselves. Knowing where this was going, Brian crossed to the group. "Good news, right?" Austin offered a half-hearted nod, as Brian shot him a smile. "Let's have a chat. Follow me."

"SOMETIMES YOU JUST HAVE TO PAY YOUR DUES."

"Austin, I know what you're thinking."

While the sounds of celebration buzzed outside the door, Austin couldn't keep the anger from exploding silently across his face. Brian reached into a cabinet behind his desk, pulling out a bottle of 30-year single malt. "You think you can't trust me, that I did something shady and back-handed by taking credit for the pivot you came up with."

Austin replied through thinly-veiled coldness, "Yeah, *something like* that."

Brian set two cut-crystal tumblers on his desk, gave each a generous pour. "This scotch is worth three thousand dollars a bottle. Do you want to know why you're drinking it in here with me, instead of drinking cheap champagne out there with everyone else?"

Austin eyed the scotch, clearly conflicted. No answer. Brian continued, "Because without you, this wouldn't be happening. However, today was about a lot more than just you. It was about our department moving forward together, and for that to happen the way it just did, I had to be the one doing the moving. If Hank saw it any other way, all our momentum, and all *your* hard work on the idea, would be for nothing."

"But why?!" Austin spit out, "Why would it be so hard for the higher-ups to accept that this idea came from someone in their twenties? Pick any business magazine today, and there are twenty-somethings on the cover changing the world!"

"A, this isn't Silicon Valley. This is the real world, where you have to actually earn your place in the Boardroom. B, you had your idea in my department, in an office that I gave you. You work for me, so your work belongs to me. And if you want to move up here, you need to remember that."

In that moment, something clicked in Austin's face: subtle, but definitive. He straightened. "Then I'd like to talk about my future here."

"Right now?"

"Yes, right now. I think it's the perfect time. You know that this product would've been mildly successful if it weren't for me. And I can promise you that I'll keep putting in the work to motivate the team and bring solutions like this to the table regularly. I know you need a new Director in the next six months, and I think I'm a natural choice."

Brian couldn't help but chuckle. Austin was ambitious, but even for him this was brazen. "Look, Austin, it's obvious that you're an excellent worker, and you know I recognize the value you add here. But this just isn't how something like this is done."

"Why not? I know the role, and I've more than–"

"Because you've been here for eighteen months, that's why not! You're twenty-seven!There are people in this department who've done your job for six, seven years longer than you, and have never said a word about promotion."

"Probably because they've never done what I just did! You know that I'm not asking for anything I haven't already shown I can do."

"You just did! Because more important than simply paying your dues, you haven't remotely demonstrated that you fully know how to run a project like this."

Austin flushed, fighting to keep himself in check. "Look, I know how to perform the role. Everything that's been asked of me, I've already gone above and beyond."

Brian nodded, "And I'm not arguing that... but what you can't rush is navigating the subtleties and nuances of troubleshooting all the challenges you don't even know exist yet. You don't know what you don't know." Brian continued, "Austin, I'm not denying that you're crushing it functionally. But the thing is, in the next role, I need you to be *much more than just functional,* okay?" Austin fell silent, his face inscrutable.

Brian's voice dropped, friendlier now. "Look, I'll share something with you that my dad once shared with me. I know it's going to sound like some old chestnut from a bygone era, but it's worth listening to. He told me that the recipe to success is to, 'Be willing to grind. Be willing to put in the time. Keep your nose to the grindstone. Stay patient and know good things will come.' You need to understand that some things just take time. Sometimes you just have to pay your dues."

He'd intended that to sound paternal, but it was clear that Austin took it as patronizing. He nodded, and then slowly stood, polite. "Thank you for the advice. I appreciate it."

The door slammed as he walked out, leaving Brian alone. *I don't get it,* he thought. *If Kerry or I had ever would've done that, Barkley would've chewed us up and spit us out.* He chuckled, then realized with a twinge of guilt that this was the first time he'd thought of Kerry in years. How they'd left things still bothered him, though he'd never quite gathered the courage to reach out and apologize.

As he tried to shake it off, his email pinged. Ironically, it was a message from Carter Bowles, Kerry's old Marketing Manager, cc'ing a dozen Axis alumni: *"Sad news about Ed. Never thought we'd see the day."*

Brian absorbed the words that followed in shock. The obituary said, "coronary." A heart attack killed Ed Barkley? Brian tried to absorb that, and the realization startled him. It had never dawned on him that his colossus of a boss was just like him: human.

Caroline

Mist dropped over the cemetery, gunmetal-grey, as Ed's casket dropped into the earth.

Brian and a cluster of his past co-workers watched silently. The surreality that had first hit Brian seemed to have fallen elsewhere as well. To anyone who'd ever worked with him, Ed being gone was like gravity breaking. They just never thought it could happen. It was as if even now, Ed held authority over them. As if they were compelled to arrive at his funeral as spectators to his death, not as past participants in his life.

After the ceremony, a group met up at a nearby restaurant to reminisce and catch up. Despite the sober circumstances, Brian enjoyed the familiarity, reminded of better times. Deep into an 'Ed story' with the old Sales team, a familiar voice cut in…

"Do you have room for one more?" Brian turned to find a slender woman with a vibrant, youthful face that Brian knew instantly, but almost didn't recognize. He felt his mouth drop open in shock. "*Kerry?!*"

She laughed, "Hi, Brian! I actually go by Caroline now. I wanted to change it for years and finally did." Her smile was at once the same, but completely different. There was a subtle energy blazing through it that he recognized but also found completely foreign. The last time he'd seen her, she'd been so *lifeless*. This was like meeting a totally different person. Gone was the chip on her shoulder. In its place, she radiated a sense of calm and peace, glowing with grace and confidence.

Brian blinked, trying to cover his surprise, "Well, ah, the name feels like it fits."

She opened her arms, offering a hug. "It's really good to see you again, Brian."

Despite how they'd left things, he couldn't help smiling and hugging her back. It really was great to see her again. "Likewise."

"So, how are you?"

He shrugged, covering, "Great. A lot of same old, same old. How's life for you?"

"I'm doing really well. I have a lot to be grateful for."

"That's great! What are you doing now?"

"Oh, just a little consulting on the side. I spend a lot more time with the kids these days. But I'm more curious about you! Give me the scoop on Axis. What's going on over there?!" She clocked the shift in Brian's demeanor and smiled, nodding to the bar. "How about a drink, for old times' sake?"

Brian nodded and followed her, knowing he couldn't say no.

Catching Up

Time might not heal all wounds, but a Long Island and a martini helped. Brian felt the distance lessen as he filled Caroline in on Axis. "Honestly, a lot of it is pretty similar to what we went through coming up. Same battle, different year."

Caroline laughed, "It can't be that similar, can it?"

"Well, it is and it isn't." Brian paused, struggling to put into words the shift he'd felt around him. "It's strange, but sometimes I feel like a lot of what we learned coming up there together just kind of got obsolete overnight, but everyone forgot to tell me. The kids we're hiring now, they're just... I don't know, it's like they think the rules don't apply to them anymore!"

"Well, maybe they don't."

Brian caught something in her tone and leaned in, curious, "What do you mean?"

"I mean this isn't the same world we grew up in."

"Damn right," Brian nodded, sipping his martini. "Want to know what just happened to me this past week? So my top hire in the past two years is this kid named Austin. Out of high school, he had a really incredible startup in the device space that just never took off. But his loss was our gain. He's a really bright guy, ambitious, killer salesman—"

"Does he remind you of someone?" Caroline's eyes twinkled as Brian laughed.

"Well, not exactly, but it's close. Anyway, last month he came up with a really smart pivot for a new product that I got the CEO and Board to sign off on. And next thing I know, he's in my office asking for a Director-level promotion! Can you believe that?! Kid's been at the job eighteen months, has one good idea, and thinks he can just start skipping steps! How entitled can you get?!" He shook his head in pure disbelief, "Can you imagine what Ed would've said if we tried something like that?"

"I don't think he would've said it so much as yelled it," Caroline grinned. "All the same, I wonder if there's a difference between entitlement and empowerment?"

"What do you mean?"

"Well, it sounds like he wasn't exactly asking for anything he wasn't at least *potentially* capable of doing. You said he came from a startup, right?"

"He did. But honestly, starting something in your garage is not the same as running projects at Axis. Besides, you've seen what happens to some people if they get promoted too early. He just hasn't earned it yet."

"But what if it's not about a title? What if what he's looking for isn't just a clear ladder to climb, so much as the reassurance that the value he provides won't be overlooked, and will be rewarded appropriately with widening circles of influence and freedom?"

Brian paused, silent, remembering the look on Austin's face in his office. Sensing his doubt, she continued. "Sometimes, money and title are far from the things that *actually* drive us, and while this new generation might be more aware of it, it's been true for a long time. Remember the Toyota case study from the early Eighties?"

"Early 80's? That's before our time!" Brian chuckled, but Caroline continued, serious.

"It was a revolutionary management shift back then, and I think it's interesting how quickly we forget. Anyway, the auto industry was getting rocked, as General Motors lost enormous market share to its new chief competitor, Toyota."

Brian, now at full attention, "Yeah, I do remember that."

"While GM plants experienced record drop-offs in quality and worker engagement, Toyota churned out higher-quality vehicles while retaining industry-high employee satisfaction ratings. GM insisted this had to do with the difference between their Eastern and Western cultures. Toyota denied that completely, and even offered to prove why by reproducing their own results at an existing GM factory."

Brian nodded, intrigued despite himself. "What did they do?"

"Well, GM gave Toyota a no-win scenario: their plant in Fremont, California. It ranked lowest in vehicle quality, and even according to their own union, featured the 'worst workforce in the entire automobile industry of the United States.' Their absentee rate hung around 20%, and even when they did show up for work, many of the workers openly drank on the job and actively sabotaged the cars they were making."

"What a nightmare!"

"To most people, yes. But Toyota's management just steadily implemented the exact same structures and culture as any of their plants back in Japan. And as they predicted, within three years the Fremont plant became one of GM's most efficient, boasting a 60% higher rate of productivity than other plants while still producing higher-quality vehicles. And all with the exact same workers as before."

"What?!" Brian shook his head, "What did they do?"

"Ironically, the key to Toyota's success wasn't giving more power to management and less to workers. Instead, it was the complete opposite: they gave less oversight to managers, and more freedom to workers. Each worker was told they were a highly-valued asset whose contributions mattered greatly, and were encouraged to make suggestions about how to improve their plant's conditions or processes. And here's the thing: *every single suggestion was implemented by the new management.* 100% of them."

"How could that possibly work? That's asking for total chaos!"

"You'd think so! But what Toyota had known for decades was that with the right mix of autonomy with structure, the workers would start to self-correct the process as they became more invested in it. Sure enough, that's exactly what happened. Over time, they fell into the rhythm of constant improvement that turned the factory around."

"So you're saying I should give someone like Austin more breathing room?"

"I'm saying that autonomy matters, it's not some new hot management trend. Yes, Silicon Valley and progressive organizations like Red Hat and W.L. Gore have embraced it recently, but so did Toyota 30 years ago. It works."

Brian drained his drink, shooting back: "Maybe, but I don't think you can just hand your employees the keys to the kingdom or start making every decision by committee. Nothing would get done. Someone has to be the boss. Besides, who does that help in the long run? Certainly not me as their boss, certainly not the company, and certainly not them. These ideas always sound great in a Fast Company article, but in the real world it's different. And no offense, but the game's changed a bit since you played it last."

His barb didn't seem to faze her at all. "I'm sure it has. I just thought I'd try to help."

"Appreciate it." Brian stood, stretching. Deep down, he knew he needed to address the elephant in the room and apologize for how he left things, but he shrugged it off. "I should hit the road. It was really good to see you, though. We should do it again soon."

Caroline nodded, "I'd like that, Brian."

Their hug goodbye was decidedly cooler than their hug hello, but Brian barely noticed. Something about what she'd said wouldn't leave him alone, and he knew the quickest way to forget it was to get back to work. Then, everything would return to normal.

He couldn't have been more wrong.

"IT'S YOU."

Entering the office the next morning, Brian noticed something strange: Austin's cubicle was empty, and his desk was bare. "Where's Austin? Why's his desk empty?" Brian looked around, confused, but no one would meet his eyes. "HELLO! Where is Austin?

Finally Shannon, one of his newest reps, offered, "I think he's down in H.R."

"Why? What happened?"

She whitened. "I'm so sorry, I thought you knew... Austin quit. So did Zach Bryson and Amy Keller." She gestured to two nearby cubicles, also empty. Seeing Brian's confusion rapidly melting to anger, she offered an apologetic, "I'm sorry—" before moving off.

Brian barged down to H.R., reeling. Austin was much too smart for this. And after all Brian had done for him? He'd be insane to leave the company now. Brian couldn't help a flash of rage bursting through his fear. *Stupid kid. This better not be true...*

"Where's Austin Rhodes?!" An admin pointed him toward the conference room at the end of the hall. The door was cracked open, and the instant he saw Austin, Brian knew he was too late: there was no mistaking the stone-cold resolve in his face. His mind was made up. Still, Brian asked, "What's going on? They said you're quitting? Is that—"

"Brian, please." Sharon Wiley, the Head of HR, interrupted him, "We're in the middle of something, you can't just–"

Brian snapped, "Give us the room, Sharon. Thanks." Sharon glanced to Austin, who nodded. *It's okay.* She shuffled out, leaving them in tense silence.

Austin's eyes matched Brian's. "Yeah, it's true. Already gave my notice."

Brian scoffed, dismissive. "Why would you do that? Especially right now—"

"You really don't know?" The disbelief was thick in Austin's voice.

Brian's confusion melted as his conversation with Caroline flashed to mind. "Is this because I didn't promote you? If that's what it is, we can circle back at the end of the year. That's just a few months, and you'd be moving faster than anyone else has ever–"

"It's not that."

"Then what's the problem? I know we're taking some hits in the marketplace, but that's cyclical, trust me. It'll turn around. Plus, we'll have EpiMatix rolling out within a year, you don't want to miss that!"

Austin regarded Brian with something like pity, "You really don't get it, do you?" He took a deep breath, "You claim to be this collaborative leader who cares about your team, but the truth is you're no different from any other ego-driven exec. The 'because I said so' school of leadership might have worked for you coming up the ranks, but it doesn't fly anymore. Life's too short to work for someone like that." He shook his head. "I'm not trying to be jerk. I just think you should know that this has nothing to do with Axis. It isn't the company: <u>it's you</u>. That's why I'm leaving."

Brian blinked, stunned silent, as Austin waved Sharon back in. "I wish you the best, Brian. I'm sure I'll see you around."

Speechless, Brian stumbled out, numb with disbelief. Employees had quit before, but it was never this personal. He couldn't stop Austin's words from running on a corrosive loop inside his mind: "*It's you...* " He felt a crack rip through his world, knowing somehow that after today, he would never be the same.

Something Needs to Change

Rain slicked the road as Brian climbed in his Tesla and punched the 'home' button on his GPS. There was no spinning this. After they'd just covered the exodus of young talent in the Board Meeting, three of Axis's best young reps walked out of the building... on his watch. Whatever favor he'd earned with EpiMatix had just been erased, he could practically hear Hank's tirade already. He felt fear invade him, raw and real.

What if Austin was right? What if he wasn't the leader he saw himself as?

Ed's funeral came rushing back to mind. Every conversation he'd had with his old co-workers had centered around some war story about how more often than not, Ed had wounded them. Sure, they all had a lot to thank the man for, but at the end of the day, not a single person who'd worked with him truly missed him.

What a hollow thing that was. What a terrible reality.

Halfway home, the panic hit him. Static blasted between his ears, as a fist of pain gripped his chest, cranking his entire body into a vice of dread. He lurched within himself, fighting the urge to escape his own body, as his vision narrowed to a pinprick. Desperate, he snapped himself out of it, just as he hurtled toward a light pole. He wrenched the wheel, slamming the brakes and throwing the Tesla into a vicious whipsaw skid, tires smoking across the road, and...

CRUNCH!! The impact punched him hard into the door, as the world went black.

"What you experienced was a panic attack, Mr. Kelly."

Brian sat on a hospital bed across from the ER doctor, as a pale Heidi gripped his hand anxiously. Brian shook his head. "Are you sure? I've never had a panic attack before. It doesn't make sense..."

"Frankly, given your current health and what you've told me about your career, it's pretty much the only explanation that does. This is a serious situation and you need to face the realities. You're overweight, overstressed, and under immense pressure. Those factors can all add up to the near-total loss of physical control that you experienced. Frankly, you're lucky to be alive."

"Sure, I have a high-stress job. But that's been true for years."

"Well, what about other factors? Family drama, or a recent personal trauma?" The question cut right through him, but Brian didn't answer, just shrugged. "Whatever it is, Mr. Kelly, just know that this is a wake-up call. If you don't change some elements of your current lifestyle, this could very easily happen again."

As the doctor left, Heidi turned to Brian, her voice small and tired. "Brian... you could have died." She shook her head, emotion overcoming her. "Something needs to change. *Right now,* something needs to change."

He nodded, knowing: a lot more than just 'something' had to change. Everything did. And he knew exactly where to start.

Long Time Coming

The next week, Brian worked up the courage to make the call. He breathed a sigh of relief as it went to voicemail, about to launch into his pre-packaged apology, when the other line rang: *Kerry*. Nervous, he picked it up. Her cheerful voice crackled, "Hi Brian! How are you?"

He took a deep breath and launched into it... "Not very well, actually. That's why I called. I wanted to apologize for how I treated you when you left Axis. A couple things have happened recently that made me realize I've got some blindspots that I really need to work on. When you left the company I felt betrayed, and I let that get the better of me. That was incredibly selfish, and I'm so sorry for what I said. If you're ever in the area, I'd love to get a drink and apologize again in person."

Her voice was gentle. Accepting. "Thank you Brian, it means a lot to hear you say that. But are you okay? You said something happened?"

"Last week after I got back from Ed's funeral, half of my best team members left the company. Or I should say, they left me. Combined with Ed's funeral, it really freaked me out. I had a panic attack on the way home from work and totaled my car."

"Oh my God! That sounds terrible, I'm so sorry..."

"It's okay, just cuts and bruises."

"Pardon me for being blunt, Brian, but it doesn't sound okay."

"Yeah, maybe not." He sighed. Even over the phone she could read him. "Honestly, I'm barely hanging on here. At work, at home, it's just nonstop pressure. I feel like I'm constantly trying to keep up, and it's just not working. I don't really know where to go from here. For once in my life, I don't have the answers."

"I see." Instead of somber affirmation, Caroline's voice was bright and cheerful. "I'm sorry you're going through this Brian, but I actually think this is excellent news!"

"What?! Why would you say that?"

"Because now you can really get to work on what matters most."

"What does that mean?"

Static burst over the line, clipping Caroline's response. She finally came through, "Brian? Sorry – going through some mountains – let's get together when I'm back. Will you be at Medcon next month?"

"Of course! We have the old table and everything."

"Great! I'll send you my—" More static cut in, as the call dropped. Brian looked out over the horizon from his windows, and for the first time in a week... he smiled.

A Lot of Explaining to Do

"The world you know will change faster over the next five years than the past fifty. That's an incredible reality, but most of us think of it in a fearful way instead of with real excitement. We sell ourselves short when it comes to the future, and that needs to change." Elon Musk prowled the stage, as a packed arena hung on every word.

Brian and Caroline watched from their VIP seats along with the rest of Axis 'upper brass.' Unlike the crowds of suited attendees, Caroline wore a simple dress, and seemed entirely unconcerned with their VIP status at the afterparty. Instead, she only seemed to care about the people at the table, Brian most of all. Her trademark authenticity had deepened noticeably over the years, and while Brian knew there had to be a reason for this shift. As he was about to ask her, he felt a hand on his shoulder.

"Excuse me, could I interrupt?" Brian's face dropped as he recognized Elon Musk himself standing behind him. "Sorry, I'm wondering if I could borrow a few minutes of Caroline's time."

Caroline rose and hugged him warmly, nodding to a shell-shocked Brian, "Elon, this is my friend Brian. Brian, Elon."

The CEO's face broke into a knowing grin, "Yes! Brian, I've heard so much about you. All good, of course." He shook Brian's hand, explaining, "Caroline got us out of tough jam last month but we've got some troubleshooting left. I just need a few minutes..."

Brian's head spun as he watched them chat. Clearly, Elon only knew her as Caroline, so he couldn't have known her for very long. What had happened in the past few years? Who had his friend become? Caroline just smiled before he could ask, "I told you, I've been doing some consulting work." She scanned the packed ballroom. "Let's go somewhere a bit quieter, we can talk there."

Brian nodded, still stunned. "Good, because you've got a lot of explaining to do..."

A World at War

Compared to the ballroom, the hotel bar was silent and empty. Brian was bursting with curiosity, but Caroline just waved him off. "This isn't about me, Brian. We're here for you. And trust me, if I were to tell you, you'd get bored pretty quickly."

"I highly doubt that!"

Again, she gracefully avoided it. "Maybe not, but still: today is about you. We'll catch up on me soon enough. Now tell me what's really going on with you."

Knowing he wouldn't be getting an answer, Brian shifted gears. "All right. Honestly? I feel like I'm losing my grip on the world. I'm always playing catch-up at home. It's the same at Axis — we're just scrambling, running around like chickens with our heads cut off. We're losing clients left and right, and seem to constantly be operating from a position of lack and fear as a culture. It just feels like we've been fighting a war on all fronts and losing. Like we've been bleeding out for the past five years."

Caroline nodded empathetically, "You're not alone, Brian. I hear similar stories from a lot of people."

"Which doesn't surprise me, honestly. But what do I *do* about it?"

"That's the good news: I can help." Her smile shone with that trademark energy. "You may not recognize it, but you're in the same exact place I was when I left Axis. I had nothing left, and had to figure out how to rebuild my life on my own. Thankfully, some of those lessons can help you."

"Like what?"

"Well, let's start with some basics." She pulled a photo up on her phone, showing it to Brian. "Remember this?"

"How could I forget?" He chuckled, recognizing... "The Playbook! You kept it!?"

"It's a lot more than a memento, Brian. It was my key to unlocking all of this. Want to know why?" He nodded. "Because it no longer applies."

He cocked his head, unsure. "What? Of course it does!"

"Brian, that world we grew up in, where we learned everything we *think* we know about business and how the world works, is very different from the one we're in now. It's not always obvious, but make no mistake: there's a war going on at work today."

Brian puzzled, "A war? How so?"

"I'm talking about a war that's been going on since the beginning of time but is being amplified right now: the battle between hierarchies and networks."

"What does that mean?"

Caroline's words dropped into the propulsive cadence of a master teacher: "The Playbook, everything we learned all those years coming up the ranks at Axis, that wasn't just the basics of business. It's a whole world-view. Everything we were taught was filtered through it, and everything we did to move up reflected it. I'm talking about the world of the **Hierarchy**." She slid a cocktail napkin onto the bar, and began drawing on it. "It looks like this..." She drew the unmistakable branch-like structure of –

"An org chart?" Brian squinted, recognizing it instantly.

Caroline nodded, "Exactly. But it's not just that: instead, this represents a collection of rules, values, and expectations. And it's been so engrained in our minds that it shows up almost unconsciously in our attitudes, actions, and approach to work and life."

"How so? Give me an example."

"I'll give you a couple of simple examples. Think about our corporate language: when we'd say things like 'oh the higher-ups will be there', or 'we need to communicate that information down', 'shoot it up the chain of command', or 'she worked her way up.' I could keep going but you get the point. All of that speaks to the top-down, command-and-control view of the world that our generation grew up living in. And it's not just our companies, either.

Tapping the napkin, Caroline continued. "Historically this has been society, everything from our government institutions to our religious institutions to the local PTA... even our families. Remember how we grew up? All the authority came from the top down; 'What I say, goes', right?" Brian nodded, flashing back to Ray saying those exact words. "And along the way, we learned this unique set of rules that we all agreed to play by to get ahead. Twenty years ago when we put them into the Playbook, we called them 'guidelines,' but now I call them something else: the **Unwritten Rules of the Hierarchy**."

"Why 'unwritten'?"

"Let me put it this way: if I were to ask you how to get ahead in business, you may not be able to point to anything that existed in the employee handbook, but you could probably think back to something that you were taught directly, or lessons you picked up indirectly from watching others' behaviors being rewarded and punished, right?" Brian couldn't help nodding. "Can you think of a few?"

Without hesitation, Brian repeated Ray's mantra: "Put your head down, keep your mouth shut, work your tail off, and don't skip any steps."

"See! Didn't take you long to remember that, did it?" Brian shook his head, amazed. "That's what I mean by Unwritten Rules: we all know them and live by them, even if they've never been put down on paper anywhere."

Brian nodded, catching on. "So if this is how we came up, what's happening now? I mean aren't those timeless lessons for life?"

Caroline flipped the napkin over and kept sketching. "Technology is reshaping and distributing power in new ways. We've all seen it play out all around us, from the Arab Spring to Uber and Airbnb. We're entering an era that will be known as the age of the networks. All around us Brian, thanks to the digitization of everything, everywhere we look in our lives we are now entagled in networks. Networks of information, education, entertainment, connections, etc. And while some experts are recognizing the networks impact on marketplaces, most are unaware of the impact these shifts have had and are continuing to have on the next generations coming of age that leaders and organizations so often struggle to connect with. You see, for everyone born after 1980, they were essentially birthed into this world."

She held up the napkin, revealing a web-like configuration of lines and points between them. "Where we've seen the world like a hierarchy, they see a **Network**: an interconnected web of people, resources, ideas, and information. They see what is, in essence, a physical manifestation of the virtual world of the web. It's a world without walls, where information is free and instantly accessible to everyone and participation and access to the game is open to anyone. In this world, the rigid levels of the Hierarchy not only seem foreign but often antiquated, and in many cases completely impractical."

Brian nodded immediately thinking of his own children. "Whoa. That actually makes a lot of sense."

"Now there are two critical elements you have to understand Brian in order to get out front on this. One, this transformation is not exclusively about Millennials and Gen Z. I know you're thinking about your kids right now. It's not just about them. They were birthed into this world and are simply giving us early clues as to how we will all operate in the network. By paying attention to some of the "networked behaviors" they exhibit, it'll will help us predict how we'll all be functioning in the future. Making this an us versus them thing will not serve us. Does that make sense?"

Brian nodded, "I get it. It's not just about the younger generations even though I can already see how coming of age in the network is shaping their views of the world."

Caroline smiled, "You got it! Number two; this world is operating by an entirely different set of unwritten rules, the **Unwritten Rules of the Network**. And those Unwritten Rules often clash in direct opposition with the world of the Hierarchy, leading to the whiplash that we all seem to have experienced at some point in the past few years."

Brian shifted in his seat sensing the enormity of it all. "So what are some of the Unwritten Rules of the Network?"

Sitting up in her chair, Caroline smiled. "I'll give you three quick ones to start. The first is what I call **Unprecedented Access**. The Network has vastly increased the volume of information to which everyone has access, resulting in elevated expectations for truth, transparency, and openness. The second, is **Exponential Reach**. The idea that anyone can contribute and participate. The barriers to entry have never been lower.

That's why you see 15 year olds starting companies and getting funding for ideas. They can push an idea out in to the world that you and I would have never been able to at that age, and as a result they expect to contribute and participate when we perhaps think they haven't earned it yet. Third: **Hyper Immediacy.** It's an instantaneous world that by it's very nature exposes the inefficiencies of the Hierarchy, a world where speed and disruption and the next iteration are not only embraced but encouraged."

Brian blinked, blown away. "How have I never heard of this before?"

A Timeless War

"You have, you may just not have recognized it that way." Slipping into the zone, Caroline kept rolling, "Think about how this war plays out at an organizational level. Hierarchies operate through scarcity, so all information and power are hoarded. Everything is a zero-sum game. Remember what Neil always said? 'If someone's winning, someone else is losing.' Thus, power is consolidated at the top of a hierarchy, and is held in place by title, rank, and authority. A network, on the other hand, is an open system that relies on the autonomy of each member to survive and thrive. Power is spread equally throughout the organization, leading to exponentially faster communication and rapid empowerment to face the shifts of culture or industry. This is why networks often survive the forces that destroy hierarchies."

"Because hierarchies are often too top-heavy to adapt?"

"Exactly. Now, think about this dynamic. Does it remind you of any recent headlines?"

Brian nodded as it hit him. "The Umbrella Revolution... Arab Spring... the Occupy Wall Street movement..."

"Yes! They're all clashes between hierarchies and networks. It's happened all throughout human history. As cultures, nations, or businesses grow in power, that power naturally tends to solidify as a hierarchy. Monarchies, dictatorships, or oligarchies are all based on this. But while hierarchies have some distinct advantages, over time they become prone to disruption. The flow of information in a hierarchy makes them obsolete when they're met with a network."

Brian nodded, catching on. "Like the music industry's fight against piracy…"

"Of course. Or if you want to go a bit further back, the Catholic Church vs. the printing press. In the 1500's, the Catholic Church controlled much of the knowledge in Western civilization. Most people couldn't read Latin, and had to rely on the Church to interpret the Bible, along with many other books. And because the cost and tools needed to reproduce a book were prohibitively high, the Church cornered the market on knowledge. But then, like it always does, disruption changed the game forever."

"I think I know where this is going: the printing press, right?"

"Exactly. Johan Gutenberg invented movable type, and suddenly any book could be mass-produced for popular consumption. This introduced mass communication to the Western world, permanently altering the structure of society. The flow of information and resulting increase in literacy eroded the pre-existing power structures, leading humanity out of the Dark Ages."

Brian nodded, his mind on fire. "I can't believe I never knew this stuff before!"

"Until six years ago, neither did I!" She smiled. "Brian, you're not a bad leader, at heart. You just have some bad habits. The leftovers of the Hierarchy aren't easy to shake, and I've spent six years of trial and error breaking those habits and re-forming everything I've learned and known about the world so that I can help people like you, people like *us*, navigate the half-changed world we live in."

Brian's brow furrowed, "Half-changed?"

"Yes. That's the big secret: the networked world is emerging, but the structures and culture of the Hierarchy still exist, and the war between the two plays out every day. The solution to moving forward isn't to just write off the Hierarchy as a whole, or totally ignore the Network. Instead, I think the organizations, businesses, and leaders who succeed in the next decade are going to be those who can find the sweet spot between the two, and lead effectively from the center-out."

Brian nodded, a bit overwhelmed. "So, what do I do now? Where do I start?"

"The good news is you've already begun. Just by seeking this conversation out, you're already ahead of the game. You're becoming conscious of this transformational shift."

"Sure, consciousness is great and all, but I have to figure out how to implement this back at work before I run the division off a cliff!"

Caroline just smiled, "Don't worry, I'll make sure that doesn't happen. But I have to warn you, this won't be easy. It may take years, and there's no guarantee you'll keep your job. In fact, if you follow what I teach you, you might lose it pretty quickly. But what good is a job that's killing you? If you want lasting solutions, I can help. If you want a quick fix, I can't."

Brian paused. Part of him didn't want to believe her, but another part of him knew he had to. All those years at Axis, and she'd always been right. Why stop trusting her now? He nodded, "What do you need from me?"

"Here's my offer: I'll lay out the road map to shift yourself and your division into this new world of work and leadership, and to coach you through the solutions as you need them. All I need to know from you is that you'll give me everything you've got."

"You know that won't be a problem for me!" He nodded, resolved. "I'm in."

The Blinders are Off

"Those words changed my life," Brian remembered. "Things were never the same after that." He tied off a bag of compost, heaving it onto the wooden cart that he and Augie would use to haul it to the long sheds where the monks undertook one of their main businesses: growing shiitake and white oyster mushrooms.

Next to him, Augie leaned on his shovel. "How so? What changed?"

"Once the blinders were off, there was no going back. That next month was like walking into a different world. Everywhere I looked, I saw evidence of the Hierarchy and Network at war in the world around me."

Augie nodded in agreement, "It's a big shift, once you get it."

"But I needed a lot more than just head knowledge in order to transform my life. Thankfully I was willing to try just about anything."

"Let me guess: she started you off with the Five Pillars?"

Brian's eyebrows rose. "Yeah... how did you know?"

Augie chuckled, a twinkle in his eye. "Who do you think taught her?"

Brian laughed, "Well, then you know what comes next."

5 Pillars of Transformation

Brian couldn't help but smile as he walked back into Bentley's. This was where it all began. And now, in that same corner booth where they'd shared so many milestones and setbacks, he and Caroline would once again mastermind the future.

"So where do we start? I'm ready!"

"So am I! Before we begin, though, I want to make sure to establish something: this isn't just about strategies and tactics, Brian. In fact that's the problem with most approaches to tackling the war at work; they're tactical, rather then existential. They're just light jabs instead of a knockout punch. If you want real change, you have to put in real work." She pulled out a napkin and starting writing. "There are five pillars of transformation every organization and leader must master in order to bridge the gap between the worlds of the Hierarchy and the Network."

On the napkin she wrote: **Heart Posture. Mindset. Culture. Process. Technology.**

"Each of these areas must be addressed in order to evolve, embrace the new world of work, and start leading from the center. Unfortunately, everyone typically jumps right to process and technology, then calls it a day. They implement the latest social platform or mobile enhancement, streamline a process or two, and think it's going to break down the silos, breathe life into the business, and prepare them for the future. Six months later, the tools are either abandoned or unused, and transformation is missed."

Brian nodded, "That sounds exactly like our collaboration platform. Actually, it sounds like most of the collaboration platforms at most of the companies I've heard of."

"Have you ever wondered why that is? And before you answer, it's not just a generational thing. I've seen executives older than you transform their careers and companies by using the exact same tools that fail at places like Axis."

Brian shrugged, "Then you've got me. How do they make it work?"

"Simple. They put first things first." She smiled, seeing Brian's confusion. "There's a quote by C.S. Lewis that I love. He said that 'when we put first things first, second things aren't suppressed: they increase.' Technology and process are important, but they're not first things. Without the right heart posture, mindset, and culture, they fail. Let me ask you something. Have you ever used Axis's platform to share something?"

Brian chuckled, "Me? No, sharing pictures of my lunch isn't exactly my thing."

"How about just sharing what you're working on? What you're worried about? What you're doing for fun? What you're reading?"

Brian shot back, "A, I don't have time for that. And B, why would anyone care?"

"Brian, talent today has different expectations for leadership. They expect more from those they follow. People care about what you share because they want to feel connected to the organization, to its mission, and to you. They want to know that you're a human being that they can relate to!"

"Caroline, c'mon. Did you ever feel like you needed to be more connected to Ed? To 'relate' to him better? Give me a break. And I highly doubt my people want to get that close to me either! I'm their boss, not their friend."

Caroline let his words hang there for a moment. "Brian, think about what you just said. That is *exactly* why organizations and leaders fail when they start this journey by tackling technology first. Axis can implement every new network-infused tool and platform under the sun, but until leaders like you put first things first and shift their mindset, heart posture, and culture to embrace the new world of work, the organization and its leaders will never truly unlock their potential."

Brian shifted, swallowing the urge to lash out defensively. Caroline noticed, softening. "I'm not trying to make you feel bad, Brian, but you came to me. And I told you this wouldn't be easy. I can't help you if you turn every lesson into an argument."

"You're right. I'm sorry. I don't even know why I fired back like that. It's almost like a reflex. Like I have to defend all the ways we've been doing things."

Caroline took a sip of her cocktail, "And you're not alone. We all have so much invested in the way things are and the way we learned to show up. It takes a tremendous amount of awareness and courage to work through this, but I know you have it in you."

Brian nodded, re-orienting himself. "Let's do it."

Caroline tapped on the napkin, "Heart Posture. Mindset. Culture. Process. Technology. I'll walk you through each of these and give you specific tools and techniques to implement back at the office. But I'm warning you now, you're going to meet resistance. When you start making these changes, you're going to make people uncomfortable."

"How should I respond?"

"Brian, it's important to come at this from a place of openness. This new leadership ethos is not a better way, it's merely *another* way. In fact, when tackling this tension between the Hierarchy and the Network, there is no such thing as right or wrong, better or worse. There's only what works and what doesn't, given what you are trying to do."

Brian smiled, "The trick is agreeing on what you're trying to do!"

Caroline laughed, "Isn't that the truth! Trust me, we'll get there. And given where you and Axis are at, I'd like to start by tackling Mindset first. But before we do, I have an exercise I want you to work on."

"Of course! What do I need to do?"

"I know you say you're 'all in,' but I also know that regardless of your intention, you're going to face internal resistance. So as we work through this process together I want you to keep coming back to these five action items. I learned a version of these statements while on a spiritual retreat with Neale Donald Walsh and have adapted them to the world of leadership. They've served me well every time I've navigated a change in my life. Hang them on your office wall. Keep them in your desk. Capture them in your phone. Keep them with you always."

1. **Permit** yourself to acknowledge that some of your old beliefs about leadership and work no longer serve you.
2. **Explore** the possibility that there are some things you do not fully understand about this new leadership environment.
3. **Announce** that you are willing for new understandings and that could produce powerful change.
4. **Courageously** examine these new understandings and if they align with your personal truth, enlarge your belief system to include them.
5. **Express** your leadership as a demonstration of your highest beliefs.

"Keep these close. Give yourself space and time to think on them. You're going to have to own and implement each one. This is where it all begins, and I believe in you."

Brian breathed deeply, feeling the weight of the moment. "I've got my marching orders, then. When can we meet up to discuss Mindset? Next week?"

Caroline just laughed, "I'll be on the other side of the country next week. But I'll be back the month after. I'll give you a call."

Brian nodded, fighting curiosity. What did Caroline do that had her traveling so much? He shrugged it off, just thankful that she was helping him. He knew he'd be fighting an uphill battle, and he was grateful for the help.

THE HUMBLE MINDSHIFT

"What can I get you two?"

Brian raised a finger as Caroline slid in across from him, "I'll just do a water, thanks!"

"Make that two." Caroline smiled, turning to Brian. "No martini tonight?"

He shook his head, "Trying to cut back every now and then. The crash was a wake-up call in more ways than one. I need to get back to the slim and trim Brian of 1994!"

Caroline nodded, pride in her eyes. "And I can't wait to see it! You know, I've seen this happen time and again: mindfulness in one area tends to spill over into others."

Brian nodded, "Speaking of which, I've been using those five action items you left me with last time, and boy were you right! No wonder every change initiative and cultural transformation we've attempted at Axis has been futile. They've all been jabs, not knockout punches! We're fiddling around the edges versus rolling up our sleeves and doing the hard work. As leadership, I don't think we've ever actually sat down and contemplated or committed to working on statements like the ones you gave me. We've never once gone deep and asked the tough questions of ourselves."

She raised a brow, "Imagine if you had?!"

Brian shook his head, "I don't know if it would work, honestly. I think most of our leaders would shrug it off as either too soft, or not strategic enough. Just like you said, we always want to default to the latest tactics, technologies or processes, instead of considering that we might be the ones who need to evolve and transform first."

"Do you ever wonder why that is?"

Brian paused, thinking. "Honestly? Pride. Ego. We don't want to be wrong."

"Yes!" Caroline glowed, pulling out her journal. "You know, this is exactly what I wanted to cover tonight: the first element of Mindset, **Humility**. Everything we're talking about ties back to the fact that the hyper-competitive environment of the Hierarchy often creates an atmosphere of self-celebration and ego inflation. We all bought into the idea that in order to stand out, you must project extreme self-confidence. We all learned to, 'Never let them see you sweat' and 'Never say, I don't know.' But history has shown us time and time again the perils of hubris."

"Hubris? It's been a while since I heard that one. Remind me what it means again?"

Caroline took a sip of water, "The word comes from the Greeks and means extreme pride and arrogance. It points to a loss of connection to reality that creeps in when those in power overestimate their capabilities. Remind you of anyone we worked with?"

"I can think of a few. But I can see both sides. To lead well, you need to be the smartest person in the room, right?"

"Sure, that's what the Hierarchy says. But what happens when that's not the case? What happens when your freshly-hired Sales Rep corrects you in a sales meeting?"

Brian whitened, flashing back to the scene she was referencing. "'Never again.' That's all Ed said, but it's all he needed to. That look on his face… I'm lucky I'm still alive!"

"Exactly!" Caroline chuckled at the memory. "But that's the Unwritten Rule, right? Never question authority. Always make your boss look good. But that environment fed off the expectation that leadership *must* be right, all the time." She leaned in further, "But fast forward 20 years into our careers, and you start to see how unconsciously we were made to believe that now that we're the leaders, we must have all the answers."

"And having all the answers makes it impossible to say, 'I don't know.'"

"Right! But think about the fact that most of us have also seen evidence that exhibiting humility, being the person who admits their flaws, actually inspires loyalty. The action actually helps to build and sustain a cohesive and empowered culture."

"Sure, but as a leader, you have to project confidence. If people start questioning your competence or ability, you'll lose control. Without a backbone, you'll get steamrolled."

"This isn't about being meek or timid, Brian. You can be strong without being overly forceful. You can be highly competent and thoughtful at the same time. You can fight for your ideas while still maintaining a posture of humility. This is why I think embracing the **Humble Mindset** is the only place to start when it comes to real transformation. By being humble, you embrace the possibility of growth."

Brian nodded, mulling it. "So, what does humility mean within the context of the Unwritten Rules of the Hierarchy?"

"One of my favorite quotes is from Lao Tzu: 'All streams flow to the sea because it is lower than they are.' Humility gives the sea its power. So we're talking about the total opposite of the Hierarchy. Instead of 'moving up' and being 'on top,' humility seeks to gain power by doing the opposite: getting low."

"No wonder it's so misunderstood." Brian's forehead furrowed, "So how do I use this? Give me something practical."

"C'mon, 'go be the sea' was a little too esoteric for you?" They both chuckled, as Caroline continued, "Fine. Here's some homework to think about and implement over the next ninety days before we meet again."

Get Low

Caroline jotted down three lines in her notebook and twirled it around toward Brian.

"Listen to me Bri, of all of the great thinkers out there dissecting the future of work and leadership, Gary Hamel is by far one of my favorites. What I'm sharing with you know I learned from him at our last jam session and I think they fit perfectly with our conversation around Humility."

"Wait what?!" Brian shook his head. "You know Gary Hamel the famous author and professor?"

Caroline smiled.

"I need to stop being surprised when you tell me your hanging with brilliant famous people!"

Caroline laughed, "Just be glad I'm sharing all their secrets with you! These are my favorite tips when it comes to getting low!"

Number 1. Embody a Spirit of Service. "Talent today quickly figures out which leaders are actually committed to helping them learn and grow, and which are just scrambling for a promotion with little regard for anyone else. Be an example to your people that those who help the most people around them get ahead, ultimately win. Your goal for the next ninety days is to help two people get promoted or reach personal milestones."

Number 2. Listen, even to the least experienced perspectives. "Start tapping into the collective consciousness of your team. You have access to so much creativity and perspective sitting under the surface of your people.

However, you can only genuinely draw it out when you're not convinced that your idea is or will be better than someone else's. Trust me, there's plenty of research that shows that the most ingenious and valuable ideas often come from those with the least experience, or from individuals who may not hold an exalted position in the organization. In fact, their very location on the fringes is what allows them to see things those in leadership may not. Seek those inputs out. I want examples when we meet again."

Number 3. Embrace Dissent. "Dissent has traditionally been rooted out in most organizations. We want to do the opposite. We want to *seek* it out. We want to, as everyone in the Valley says, disrupt ourselves. On every important issue, we as leaders should ask our people and colleagues, 'Where do I have it wrong?' or 'What would you do differently?'"

Brian shook his head, giving himself a reality check. "Look, it's easy to talk about asking those questions, but doing it is whole other issue. Why is it so hard?"

Caroline smiled, "Ego, my friend. Ego is fed in the Hierarchy. Think about it: the corner office, the title, the Executive Parking, the Executive Dining Room. Admitting 'I don't know' doesn't belong in rooms like that! But that also doesn't make for great leadership. The best leaders I've worked with are the ones who constantly get the most opinions on the table before making a decision."

Brian nodded, "Admitting there might be a better way? I think I can do that."

"For the good of your team, you need to! The Hierarchy can really hold us back in this area, so I'm going give you a really specific exercise to work on for this. One of the reasons we shut down alternative approaches is because it often runs counter to an unwritten rule that's been engrained in us. So I want you to consider… '*What's One Unwritten Rule You Want To Help Your Org Let Go Of?'* What's something you know in your gut no longer serves you, the culture, or the company?"

"Can you give me an example to help me start thinking about it?"

"Of course! I recently asked that question to a room full of executives in the financial services space and had them share a few. This powerful woman stood up and admitted, 'The unwritten rule I want to let go of is: 'When people aren't in their desk, it means they are NOT working.'"

Brian nodded, "Whoa! I think that's one of mine, too!"

Caroline nodded, "I see a lot of leaders struggle with the idea of workplace flexibility. Because in our day, we needed to be physically present to do our jobs. So to us, if we don't see someone physically present at their desk, of course they *must not* be working!"

Brian nodded. "Why do we assume people need to be watched over like children? Why not just set clear expectations, clear consequences, and then treat them like adults and let them just go get the job done?"

Caroline smiled, "Now who's the teacher?" He just laughed as she stood up. "Great work, Brian. Now 'go be the sea' and I'll see you back here in ninety days!"

The Abundance Mindshift

Running behind from another thirteen-hour day, a disheveled Brian plopped down across from Caroline. "I know I know, I'm sorry. But before we jump in, I need to tell you a story. I ran into an old friend last week: Neil Hackworthy."

"Neil! How is he?" Caroline smiled.

"Oh, he's still Neil. Anyway, in the process of catching up, I told him everything we covered last session. About the value of getting low, staying humble, and not getting caught up in the self-aggrandizing race to the top like everyone else."

"Good for you! How'd he respond?"

"He thought I was nuts. 'Brian, are you joking? If you want to succeed, someone above you has to pick you, and to get picked you have to be a star. You don't become a star by 'getting low,' you do it by being visible, by winning and making sure people see it.'"

Caroline couldn't help but smile. "Neil never was a very low-profile guy."

"Oh, it gets better. He then very confidently told me that he only has two rules to getting ahead. The first is, 'Don't tell anyone what you know.'"

"Of course." Caroline's smile grew, "And the second one?"

"He just laughed and said, 'Obviously, I can't tell you.' How good is that?!"

Caroline couldn't help but chuckle, "I can see him saying that right now!"

"Right?! It reminds me of his other one, 'There are only so many spots on the bus.' One of our first Unwritten Rules."

"And one of the most foundational. It changes the way you look at absolutely everything. But let's think about 'don't tell anyone what you know' for a second. What do you gain by doing that?"

Brian paused, thinking. "Well, for one, security. The thinking is that my holding on to this information actually keeps me safe. Because if I know this trade, this skill, this program, and no one else does, then there's one thing I know you can't do: fire me."

Caroline smiled, "That's it! On top of which, you gain the power that comes from control. Because if you know something no one else does, people have to come to you for the answer. Knowing that thing gives you power and influence over others."

"But only if you keep it to yourself," Brian mused.

"Exactly. We were taught that power came from hoarding information. But things are different now. Power comes from sharing, not hoarding today." Brian nodded, writing the sentence in his notebook as she continued, "We're living in the sharing economy. The way to gain influence now is to actually *give away* your best content and expertise."

Brian shook his head, "It's the total opposite of how we were conditioned to operate!"

Caroline nodded, "'There are only so many spots on the bus.' That Rule taught us all to live with a **Scarcity Mindset**. We learned that there's not enough to go around. Not enough positions, promotions, time, budgets, you name it. There are limited resources out there, and if you want them, you've got go out and fight for them."

Brian nodded, realizing just how deeply this had impacted him. "And once you do get them, don't let them go. Operating from that position makes you hold onto everything."

"Unfortunately, most leaders don't realize just how damaging a scarcity mindset can be for a company's culture." Caroline shook her head. "Instead, the world of the Network embraces the opposite: the **Abundance Mindset**, which understands that there is always more than enough to go around. More than enough resources, talent, creative ideas, more than enough 'spots on the bus.'"

Brian paused, thrown. "But doesn't that kill competition?"

"Of course not. It's not about just sitting back and waiting for the abundance to pour in without any effort. Instead, the Abundance Mindset recognizes that while there will always be fresh talent coming up, there's also always space for you, because no one is exactly like you. It's on you and you alone to work hard, pour your passion into your craft, and ensure that you're always presenting the best version of yourself."

Brian seemed unconvinced. "It's hard to embrace. Especially when the reality you're facing is not an abundant one. We're looking at real scarcity at Axis right now."

Tapping on her temple, Caroline leaned in, "You create your reality here first. It's all about perspective. You can embrace an abundant mindset with very little."

"What do you mean?"

"Have you ever met someone who appears to have very little, but lives a full and abundant life? Or someone who appears to have everything, yet still lives like it's never enough?" Brian nodded, as she continued, "Have you ever wondered why that is?"

He shrugged, as she continued, "It's a choice, Brian. It's always a choice. And the implications are huge. I'm sure we can find organizations that have 'less' than Axis but are able to do more. They don't allow their perceived lack of resources and talent to hold them back. Instead, they lean into the idea that they always have more than enough to accomplish their individual and collective missions."

"Got it," he replied. "So, the million-dollar question: how can I shift my division to be more like that?"

Caroline smiled, "One word: **gratitude**."

The Scarcity-Killer

"The most effective way to help the culture at Axis embody the Abundance Mindshift is to embrace it yourself, by leveraging the power of gratitude. Because while comparison feeds scarcity, gratitude kills it. It's impossible to feel 'less than' when you focus on what you're grateful for. See, life has a tendency to show up the way you expect it to. It reflects back to us what we've given it to work with, and by focusing on all that we're grateful for, we give it more abundance to reflect back. It's a practice that kills scarcity and grows fulfillment, you just have to do it every day."

Brian leaned in, curious, "Wait. How do I make gratitude something I 'do' every day?"

"I'll give you two specific actions I want you to implement over the next 90 days that will help you lean into this. Step One, is to get your morning routine dialed in."

"My morning routine? You mean not hitting snooze five times?!"

Caroline chuckled, "It's a bit more than that. For the purposes of this exercise, I want you to use a little book called 'The 5 Minute Journal.' Like the name implies, it asks you to take five minutes each morning to answer these questions...

I am grateful for...
What would make today great?
Daily affirmation. I am becoming....

"You write down three answers for each. More often than not, I go a lot longer than five minutes. But just that simple act of consistent focus on gratitude each morning has revolutionized my outlook, my focus, and my capacity for gratitude in life."

Brian sat back and took a deep breath. "Wow. You start every morning like that?"

"Well, it doesn't have to stop there. The 5 Minute Journal also contains two questions for each evening to wrap up your day with gratitude as well."

What are three amazing things that happened today?

How could I have made today better?

"So that's Step One, which covers how to step into the abundant mindset personally. Step Two focuses on bringing abundance to your professional life and embed it in the culture, and I call it 'First 5.'"

Brian cocked his head, "First 5?"

She smiled, "Absolutely. Meetings are a tremendous opportunity to influence the culture of an organization. So, at the beginning of every meeting with your team, I want you to leverage the first five minutes to focus on what's happening in the business that you're grateful for."

Brian's eyebrows rose, "What if it's a bad week? What if no one says anything?"

"Oh, it'll be hard to engage them at first. Most meetings focus on scarcity and problems, and old habits die hard. It's up to you to lead by example and steer the team's focus. Have everyone rattle off one thing happening in the business that they're grateful for. I promise you that after 90 days of this practice, you will absolutely notice a shift in the culture away from scarcity, and toward abundance." Seeing his hesitation, she added, "And if it doesn't, the bar tab for our next meeting is on me."

Brian laughed, "You're on. And I'll tell you one thing I'm grateful for right now: a generous friend who's always willing to pick up my tab!"

A smile shot across her face. "I'm grateful for you too, Brian. Now let's get out of here. You've got work to do!"

"WHERE ARE YOU?"

Inspired by his sessions with Caroline, Brian dove headfirst into putting her lessons into practice. Every week brought new realizations as he began to implement what he'd learned, pouring himself into the process of transformation.

At first, his team members seemed confused when he encouraged them to blatantly disagree with him if they thought he was wrong. But once they sensed that his invitation was genuine, the process began in earnest. Of course, his ego took more than a few hits at first, but as Brian began to see just how valuable their insights were, he became increasingly grateful for each and every one of his team members. He began meeting with many of them one-on-one in an effort to get to know them better, a rewarding but exhausting process that stretched his already-thin schedule even thinner.

Things reached a breaking point one Friday night as he and Heidi drove to a favorite restaurant for their weekly date night. As she filled Brian in on her week, he felt his phone vibrate. He silenced it, just as it another call came in. He ignored it, turning back to his wife. But as she kept talking, his mind began running through the list of potential crises that could be happening. After a minute, he blinked, coming out of it, only to realize... the car was totally silent. Heidi just staring out the window, tears streaming down her face.

Brian did his best to connect with her, "Honey? What's going on?"

She just shook her head, defeated. "Are you even listening? Where are you right now? Because it sure doesn't feel like you're here with me."

"I am! I'm sorry, it's just been another insane week at work, and I'm being pulled in a million different directions right now."

"Except for mine. I know you're under a ton of stress, but lately, sometimes I feel like even when I'm with you, I'm still alone." Her words hit Brian in the gut, as he nodded, knowing: something had to change.

"I'm so sorry, Brian. I know from experience how hard that situation is. There's nothing worse than hearing that the person you love most in the world feels alone."

Caroline cleared a lump in her throat, as Brian nodded. "Thanks. We've started to work through it, but boy was I taken off-guard. It just hit me: I have such a hard time being where I am. Between work and home, I feel like I'm constantly split in two. My phone never stops beeping. My attention span is zero. I don't know how to manage it all."

Caroline gave him a knowing smile, "Well, you're not alone. We're all struggling with the exact same thing these days. We're in the midst of the Information Age, but for all of its potential, there's a cost. Somehow the things designed to keep us constantly connected, can leave those closest to us feeling more disconnected from us than ever. Our inability to focus is a huge epidemic with a massive cost, and everyone in the modern workforce seems stuck trying to navigate it. Especially leaders."

"Exactly! How do I show up for all the people that need me both at home and at work, when our world is so complex and hyper-connected?"

Caroline nodded, "Deloitte just reported that more than one-third of executives rated this issue among their top five priorities when thinking about the future of work, but fewer than one in ten thought they were dealing with it effectively."

"So, I guess the question is: how can I be the one in that ten? How can I solve this?"

Caroline nodded, "The good news is that you're at least aware of the fact that you've stop being present, and you're noticing the impact it's having on your relationships and your effectiveness as a leader. Obviously it's a painful realization, but now that you're aware of it, we can start to work on it."

The Present Mindshift

"Brian, I want to share some secrets I started practicing a few years back that have been incredibly helpful for me, and for those I have shared them with. I call them '**The Present Mindshift**.'" Caroline retrieved her iPad from her bag, offering it to Brian. "I want to show you a short video on YouTube called 'Automatic Thoughts,' by Dr. Henry Cloud. In his best-selling book *Boundaries* he says that the present mindshift starts with creating and enforcing healthy boundaries. Let's watch…"

As they did, Brian sat mesmerized. "Yes! That's exactly what happens to me, I have these thoughts flying through my head, and when I grab onto them, just like a bird, they go crazy, and it makes me feel anxiety and frustration."

"Well, there's hope," said Caroline. "There's a technique that I want you to start practicing that will allow you get better at observing your thoughts without judging them or latching on to them, but as Dr. Cloud says, just letting them fly on by. So, I want you to start every day with gratefulness prayer and meditation."

"Meditation? Sounds intense," Brian responded. "I'm not sure I can do that."

"It's so simple, I'm certain you can. Here's what I do: I just sit in a hot shower every morning and spend three to five minutes creating a heart posture of gratitude by giving thanks for all the simple things in life that I take for granted. Things like clean drinking water, and the ability to walk, talk, and feed myself. Or a warm bed, shoes, and food. Then,

I allow myself to slip into more of a meditative state, where I simply observe the thoughts that come into my mind without judgment. If I have a big meeting that week, my mind will often go there, and I try and guide my mind into seeing myself overcoming the inevitable challenges that will come up and operating at my very best."

"I guess that could be useful," Brian admitted.

"It really is! And the beauty of doing it in the shower serves a dual purpose. First, in a hot shower our brain waves slow down and are much closer to a meditative state. Second, since I start my day in the shower no matter if I'm at home or traveling, I know I can always get it in, no matter what."

Brian nodded, "It does sound easy enough to try, at least."

"Great! Now, this next one is much more difficult. But I can promise you that it will add immense value in every single area of your life. It is going to be very uncomfortable at first, because you are going to need to create and enforce healthy boundaries."

"Well, as a very wise man once told me, 'uncomfortable and hard aren't a choice, but where you experience them is.' I'm sick of experiencing uncomfortable and hard in the wrong places, so let's have it!"

"Here it is: when you're at work, I want you to put your phone on silent at all times. I want you to carve out at least four hours per day where your office line doesn't ring and people can't interrupt you, and I want you to only handle email for thirty minutes after lunch, and thirty minutes before heading home."

"Are you serious?! I'm not sure I'll be able to get anything done that way!"

"Oh, you'll be amazed not just at *what* you'll get done, but at *how much.* Remember, when we put first things first, second things aren't suppressed, they increase. The more you practice being fully present and fully engaged in the truly important areas of your life, the more it spills over into every other area. Because by trying to be present in *all* areas of your life, you've been stretched too thin to actually be truly present in *any* of them. The beautiful thing is that when you start to live fully engaged in the present moment, you'll actually feel like you have a lot more time."

Brian nodded, but he was still struggling to grasp it. "So if I'm at the office and something urgent comes up, how is someone supposed to get a hold of me?"

"You need to redefine what words like 'urgent' mean. Most 'urgent' things can wait a few hours, or even a few days to be handled, and when you and your team start to create healthy boundaries where people cannot be interrupted except for true emergencies, you'll start to see a dramatic increase in employee engagement, productivity, and well-being. Oh, and I want your cell phone turned completely off as soon as you get home, and left off until you return to the office the next day. Whatever it is, it can wait until tomorrow."

"Doesn't that feel a little unrealistic?"

"Let me ask you something difficult, Brian. If tomorrow morning you got the very same diagnosis that your father did, and knew you had just months to live, how important would everything that's kept you from being fully present with your family really be? Or even worse, what if you lost Jameson or Ava in an accident tomorrow? How much would you regret wasting precious moments with them because of some 'urgent' email that easily could have just been handled at the office?"

Brian just blinked, taken aback by that sobering truth, as Caroline continued, "I know you think those examples are extreme, but they happen to thousands of people every day. The pain of discipline is much better than the pain of regret. Stop sacrificing what is truly important at the altar of what feels urgent in the moment. Life is precious, and you only get so much time here on earth, so make sure you are living present and focusing on what truly matters."

Brian nodded, blinking away emotion. As he regained his composure, he admitted, "I know you're right. I need to make some serious changes before it's too late. Thank you for valuing me enough to be harsh. I really needed that."

"Sometimes we all do," Caroline smiled. "Now go back to your family and start living fully present with them!"

Counterculture

It had only been a few months since Caroline and Brian had last met, but already she noticed a difference. His presence was calmer, his waistline thinner, and the lines on his face softer; he looked healthier and more well-rested than she'd ever seen him.

Caroline grinned. "You look five years younger! Did you get a little nip and tuck?"

"Not quite," Brian smirked, "But I've been catching up on a few years of missed sleep. Between that and hitting the gym, I certainly *feel* five years younger! And you were right about the morning meditation; having that dialed in has really changed things."

Caroline glowed with pride, "I'm so proud of you! Your mindset work has come a long way over the past year. Do you feel ready to move outward in your focus? I thought we could tackle the Culture Pillar today, and explore how you can start to influence Axis."

"Perfect. But before we change the world, I need a cocktail! I'm still holding off on them most days, but this feels like it's worth celebrating."

"Agreed!" Caroline flagged the server down and ordered the usual.

As they bustled off, Brian pulled out his journal and pen, and settled in. "So I have to ask something: how exactly do you define 'culture'? We talk about it all the time at Axis, but I've actually always secretly struggled to define what it is."

"No, that's a great question. You're not alone in asking it, either. Culture is tricky. It's this intangible that runs through an organization, like someone's personality and there are countless definitions out there."

Brian nodded as their drinks arrived. "No wonder it's so hard to nail down."

"It is, but tonight we're going to do just that. And keep in mind that it doesn't matter if the rest of the world has a slightly different definition, what's important is that everyone at Axis is aligned around what it means for you."

Brian sat back in the booth, "Got it. So, how would you define culture?"

Caroline grabbed her pen and started writing...

CULTURE = The formal or informal, agreed upon, attitudes and behaviors that are either rewarded or penalized inside an organization.

Brian read it over a few times, impressed, "Caroline, this is great! I think it's right on."

She smiled. "Thank you! Another way to think about it is to go back to the Unwritten Rules we've already talked about. Any organization's culture is generally made up of their own unwritten rules for working together. Think of it as 'the way we do things around here.' That in turn informs the context within which people judge the appropriateness of their behavior and how they treat one another."

Brian nodded, "I hadn't thought about it that way before, but you're right. The unwritten rules we all learned absolutely shaped the culture. In fact, some of those are probably so deeply embedded that I don't know if I can change them."

"Without a huge group of influencers joining you, that might be true. That's why for now, I just want you to focus on attitudes and behaviors, because while they're small, those are the building blocks of culture. They're where the rubber meets the road." Flipping her notebook back around, Caroline pointed at the page. "So, if you think about the Axis culture today, what are the behaviors that get rewarded?"

Brian reflected for moment, then grabbed the notebook. He drew a line down the center of the page. "What if on one side I write down all of the behaviors we want to expand and reward, and on the other side I write all of the behaviors that are currently being rewarded, but are holding us back. The ones we want to correct."

Brian's mind spun, realizing just how many detrimental behaviors and attitudes were currently being rewarded at his company. As Caroline looked on, he started to write....

Generosity | Hoarding
Transparency | Deception
Competitive | Cutthroat
Accountability | Impunity
Committed | Fickle
Adaptable | Rigid
Receptive | Close Minded
Advocate | Antagonist
Opinionated | Argumentative
We-Minded | Me-Minded

Brian sat back, satisfied, "So these are just the top ten. On the left are the positive behaviors and attitudes I want to see more of, and on the right are unfortunately the majority of what actually plays out at Axis."

"Starting with ten is a great first step, Brian. Again, the idea isn't to change things overnight, but to slowly reshape those Unwritten Rules of the Hierarchy that are negatively influencing the culture, and start to embrace the world of the Network. Identifying and calling out behaviors like this is a fantastic start." She sat back and smiled, "Let's rally back here next month, and we'll pick our top three that you want start working on in the coming months to create new culture."

"I think calling it 'counter-culture' is more accurate!"

Caroline laughed, "I think you're probably right! Here..." She quickly typed the word into her phone, reading the definition aloud. "A subculture whose values and norms of behavior differ substantially from those of mainstream society, with accompanying hope for a better life or a new society. A counter-cultural movement expresses the ethos and aspirations of a specific population."

Brian smiled, "Boom! If that's not us, I don't know what is! We're starting a movement."

"EASIER SAID THAN DONE."

"Well, as I'm sure anyone who's been in business for a while knows, that's easier said than done," Augie laughed. He and Brian were back in the vegetable garden, yanking out weeds one by one. The sun was high overhead, and sweat poured down their backs.

"That's an understatement," admitted Brian. "After almost a year of mindset work, I was seeing a lot of amazing changes personally. What Caroline taught me was genuinely beginning to transform my life, both at home and at work. I felt like a new man, with a new lease on life. Suddenly I had reserves of time, energy, and willpower that I never knew existed! But bringing that up against the entire culture of a company that had been entrenched and encouraged over decades... that's a different story."

"It is indeed," Augie nodded. "One of the most difficult realities of leading others is that change does not happen on our schedule. To allow others the room to grow at their own pace, we need to have the grace to accept timelines that are different from our own."

"One of the most beautiful things about starting on our own personal mindset first is that it gives us a healthy does of humility. If we are honest and are doing the hard work internally it should give us the patience and empathy when we start rolling it out collectively in our teams and across the company.

"Yes! And one of the hardest parts of that," Brian replied, "Was the reality that as much as I'd been able to learn and grow, I still had a long journey ahead."

"You've learned a very valuable lesson Brian! Mindset work is incredibly challenging and if the leaders don't have the patience and empathy from going through it personally, it almost always backfires.

Immigrants and Artisans

"Hey! Good timing!" Brian grabbed the door and followed Caroline into Bentley's.

Caroline smiled, noticing his energy, "You look ready to go!"

"I am! I've been looking forward to this all day." As they sat, Brian apologized, "I'm sorry, I have to pick the kids up in an hour, so I don't have a ton of time."

"Brian, you never have to apologize for putting first things first!"

"I know, I know. Old ways die hard, I guess." He smiled, "So, I've been focusing lately on the actions and attitudes that I want to see more of at Axis. I think one of the biggest ways we could improve is by fostering a greater sense of accountability and elevating expectations."

Caroline leaned in, "That's a big one! What makes you want to tackle it first?"

"Because I see it play out every day, from our new hires all the way to the top. We've become tolerant of underperformance. We either don't clearly define expectations for people, or we just fail to hold them accountable for the things they say they're going to do. And that pattern spreads like a disease. Talent sees leaders not setting or living up to expectations, without being held accountable for it. And then we wonder why we see underperformance and a lack of ownership in young talent."

Caroline nodded, "Many of the leaders I work with tell me how bad the work ethic is amongst their Millennials."

Brian let out a sigh, "But here's the thing: they're also some of my best workers. So I read these articles every week about the younger generation's lack of work ethic and commitment, and I have to say, it's just not always true!"

"I agree. And even if it sometimes is, the fault often lies squarely with their older leadership. Leaders need to clearly define what's expected, then coach and help people meet those expectations. And finally, they need to hold them accountable. If they're not stepping up, they're not the right fit and it's time to part ways. Period."

"I completely agree," Brian nodded. "But I really want to get creative with how we start to embed this in the culture. Thomas Friedman is one of my favorite writers, and he has a brilliant insight into this idea of accountability and expectations. He said, 'We're all new immigrants today to the hyper connected networked world.'"

"Interesting. And what does that have to do with expectations?"

"Everything!" Brian leaned in, "Friedman goes on to say, 'The new immigrant wakes up every day and says, 'Nothing is owed me in this world. Nothing is promised. There is no legacy spot waiting for me at IBM or Harvard. I'm not owed a job, a raise, a title bump or a promotion. I better figure out what world I'm in, understand where the opportunities are, and work harder than the next guy to achieve them.'"

Caroline's eyes lit up, "That is brilliant!"

"I know, right? But there's more. He then explores another idea from a Harvard professor named Lawrence Katz, who said workers in the digital age need to start to, as he puts it, 'think like an artisan.'"

"What does that mean?"

"Well, he reminded us that artisans as a class sprang up in the Middle Ages, before mass production. They made everything one-off: every pair of shoes, every saddle, every tool or utensil. And the artisan took such pride in their work, they brought so much extra to what they did, that they carved their initials into every piece. The idea being, whatever job you do today, at the end of every day, would you want to carve your initials into the work?"

"It's the ultimate sign of ownership. This piece of work is going to live on, and I'm going to pour myself into it in such a way that I'm proud to call it mine."

Brian couldn't contain his excitement, "Now imagine if everyone on my team brought the mindset of both an immigrant and an artisan into Axis each day?"

"It would completely transform your team! Or, the ones who couldn't get on board would gradually leave and the natural immigrants and artisans would flock to work there." Brian nodded as Caroline began to smile. "But you know there's only one way that's going to happen: it has to begin with you. I think you go back to the team tomorrow and say, 'Look, in order for us to get where we say we want to go, we have to change a few things. We have to start expecting more of ourselves and start holding each other accountable, and that starts with me."

Brian's eyebrows rose, "I can see why you covered the Humble Mindshift first! I never would have admitted that a year ago."

"But if you want true cultural change, you have to be willing to go deep and you have to be willing to go first. I would tell them, 'It starts with me because the truth is, I haven't always held myself to the highest expectations, and I haven't always been accountable for my actions. That changes today, but I need your help. I want you to hold me accountable to what I say I'm going to do. I'm empowering you to *call me up* to a higher level if you see me not living out the standards and ideals we've all agreed upon.'"

Brian sat back as her words hit him. "Wow… you're not making this easy."

"I told you it wouldn't be," she pressed. "Bringing genuine transformation isn't something you can fake, Brian. If you want your people to start operating like immigrants and artisans, where nothing is owed and every piece of work is so valuable that it's worth signing your name to, you have to do the same. You have to go first."

"I have to be willing to sign my work as a leader." He chuckled, "Even if it makes me feel like a stranger in a strange land!"

Mission Matters More

"Do you know what separates a good company from a great one Brian?"

"Well according to Jim Collins…"

Caroline's eyes narrowed, "Ha. You know most of those companies they featured in that project are no longer in business right?"

"I know. Crazy. Probably a lesson to be learned there."

Caroline sat back and crossed her arms, "I wonder how many were stuck in the hierarchy and got blown up by the network?"

Brian smiled, "Too bad they didn't have you around!"

"Ha! Right!? Now back to my question, what separates the good companies from the great ones today?"

Brian scratched his head, "I don't know, I think it's a number of things but something we always talk about at Axis is the importance of measuring results and effective goal-setting."

Caroline smiled. "I thought you'd probably say that given it was drilled into our heads over and over again by leadership, and I'll admit I believed it for a long time. But the life of Mother Theresa and the Trappist monks made me totally reconsider it."

"Mother Theresa?"

"Yes, Mother Theresa. She never had a goal, but she did have a mission that acted as her internal gps system. Her mission was to serve the needs of the sick and the dying. Now, let me ask you a question, can anyone ever stop you from serving the needs of the sick and the dying?"

Brian thought for a moment. "No, I don't believe so."

"Exactly!" Exclaimed Caroline. "When we live a mission driven life there is only one person responsible for whether or not we live it out. The person staring back at you in the mirror."

"I think that is why so many people like goals, because goals actually allow them to shift the responsibility onto someone else's shoulders. There are a lot of people and organizations that can place roadblocks in the way of someone becoming a doctor, but no one can stop you from serving the needs of the sick and the dying."

"I guess I hadn't thought about it like that before." Said Brian.

"Now the idea of having a mission statement that matters isn't new. People have been talking about this forever, especially as the next generation of talent has entered the workforce over the past decade. I remember talking about the trend of mission and meaningful work being more important than money to Millennials and people laughing at me. What they didn't understand was the difference between having a lifeless mission statement that hangs on a wall somewhere and being an authentically mission driven organization and how infusing that into the dna of every decision made in the company could have a transformational affect on the culture."

Brian responded, "We do have a mission statement at Axis."

"Of course you do Brian, everyone does. Enron had a mission statement too."

Caroline pulled up a quick Google search for Enron's mission statement and slid her phone across the table.

Enron's motto was "Respect, Integrity, Communication and Excellence." Its "Vision and Values" mission statement declared, "We treat others as we would like to be treated ourselves....We do not tolerate abusive or disrespectful treatment. Ruthlessness, callousness and arrogance don't belong here."

Brian just shook his head as he read. "That's wild, it meant absolutely nothing! Its just words."

"Exactly Brian! That's why we have to go beyond mission statements, or core values statements, I'm talking about a mission that is embedded in the hearts and minds of every person in the company, but especially those in leadership positions so that it gets passed down and embedded inside of everyone overtime. Your mission needs to be infused into the core of your company so deeply that it is the internal gps system for guiding every action taken in the company!"

"Why do you think you do what you do Brian? Why do you think Axis exist?"

"Is it bad if I say to honor our obligations to shareholders?"

"It's not about good or bad, right or wrong Brian but I do think it's interesting to think about whether or not that's what you want your life to be about. Is that why you're putting in crazy hours and missing time with family? To ensure shareholders earn a solid return?"

"I was partially joking Caroline. Obviously we have a responsibility to investors but we do what we do to improve people's lives."

"Yes! And when that becomes the true north for you personally and for Axis collectively, then you won't need to worry about creating a solid return for investors, because it will come as a natural byproduct of an authentic mission driven organization. The same way the Trappist monks always create highly successful businesses, because they are focused on fulfilling their mission not profit." Caroline finished with a big smile on her face.

Brian thought for a minute as he was trying to fully digest it. "I'm just not sure many people have the stomach for it."

"Exactly Brian! And ironically that's wherein lies the greatest opportunity! My challenge to you is to find ways to continually keep the mission front and center of peoples activities and action. Whenever you're making a decision I want you to ask, does this serve the needs of our customers? Is this improving their lives? Does this represent the values that we've set forth to drive our actions? If it does, do it. If it doesn't, don't. Period. The more consistent you are in your actions and behaviors around this the more it will be embraced by those that you're leading."

Brian stood up to leave and with a smile on his face fired back, "Leaders go first."

Encouraging Dissent

As the months passed, Brian's resolve to see true transformation in his personal and professional life was tested again and again. But as he applied his newfound mindset, attention, and energy to each challenge, he began to see real changes not only in how he showed up for those around him, but also in how they showed up for the organization and their clients. But while his team was revolutionizing themselves, it was 'business as usual' for the rest of the company. The culture of low expectations, blame, and hierarchical leadership kept most workers disengaged, or worse, running for the exits.

"Our turnover has never been higher. I don't know how much longer it can go on," Brian admitted to Caroline one night at Bentley's. He sighed, "But I know we're not here to talk about that tonight."

"That's right, my friend," Caroline smiled, "Tonight we're here to tackle the final chapter of what I can teach you."

Brian reacted, confused, "Final chapter? But I have so much more to learn!"

"In many ways, yes. The internal work you've begun, that will never stop. But as far as helping you navigate the half-changed world of work, my job is nearly done. You've made incredible progress. You've let countless Unwritten Rules go, embraced mindset shifts, and started the heavy lifting of transforming the culture around you."

Brian sighed, "I appreciate that, but I know I still have so much to work on! I still find Unwritten Rules that no longer serve us creeping up on me. I still wonder if I'm really doing this right."

"And that's not a bad thing. I call it the caterpillar effect." She laughed at the look on Brian's face. "When caterpillars become butterflies, they retain memories of their days as a caterpillar in their neuroreceptors. So even though they've totally transformed, they still bump up against those old memories. As humans, we often do the same thing. Even after we've grown and changed so much, old memories of who we used to be still make us feel like imposters. It's normal. Stay the course."

Brian chuckled, "You're dropping caterpillar knowledge on me now!" Caroline laughed and pulled her notebook out. "Now, our last lesson in transforming culture is, 'Encouraging Dissent.'" She paused as a slow smile grew over Brian's face. "What's wrong?"

"Nothing! I'm just remembering the night in this very booth where you wanted to fire Kevin Walker, just because he was pushing back on your decisions. Ironic, right?"

Caroline rolled her eyes, "Kevin Walker! Boy did he know how to make my blood boil!"

Brian started to laugh, "He had, what did you call it, 'no respect for the party line?' Which was unacceptable, because —"

"—insubordination can't be tolerated!" Caroline couldn't help but smile. "And look, maybe Kevin's insubordination truly didn't deserve to be tolerated, but I've since learned that of all the Unwritten Rules, that might be the most damaging to an organization as a whole."

"I'm starting to see why," Brian agreed. "The more I commit to getting low and embracing the Humble Mindshift, the more I realize the value of questions and statements that the Ed Barkley's of the world would never embrace. Things like 'I'm sorry.' 'I don't know.' 'I was wrong.' Or, 'How would you do it differently?'"

"You're really catching on!" Caroline glowed. "Are you sure I'm the one teaching here?"

Brian waved her off, "I just care about my division, and I know we're not going to survive without fully unleashing everyone's wisdom, knowledge, and perspective. I honestly can't do this on my own. I can't be solely responsible for every great idea and innovation we implement. The world is changing too fast for that!"

"You're exactly right. Ed Catmull, one of the founders of Pixar, once said, 'If there is more truth in the hallways than in the meetings, you have a problem.' And he puts his money where his mouth is, too. Did you know that Pixar's directors screen their films as works-in-progress for the entire company up to a dozen times during production, and allow absolutely anyone, from the assistants to the catering workers, to give notes?"

Brian whistled, amazed. "No wonder their movies are so good! It makes so much sense though. I'm convinced the best leaders today are the ones who get the most opinions on the table before making a decision. Of course they still make the final call, and the buck still stops with them, but they're relentlessly committed to being open. "

"As opposed to what we learned, which was to squash any kind of dissent. But despite its bad connotations, 'dissent' simply means 'to hold or express opinions that are at variance with those previously, commonly, or officially expressed.' The problem is that those previously-held views can be just plain wrong, and at the speed of the networked world, they often will be. Without dissent, innovation is impossible!"

Brian shook his head, "But because it threatens the Hierarchy, it's blocked. Think about how many policies are in place at any given company purely to preserve the fiction that the higher-ups are really in control? Or how many rules enforce standardization at the expense of initiative and passion? It's got to stop!"

"And I have a feeling that it will," Caroline chuckled. "At least in your division."

"Oh, I already started." Brian grinned, pulling up the Notes app on his iPad. "I told you I've been thinking about this a lot lately. I jotted a few ideas down earlier this week when I was thinking about how to 'disrupt' our division before our competition could."

"I told you, my work is done here!" Caroline laughed. "What did you come up with?"

In response, Brian turned around his iPad, revealing three ideas...

1. Be Open

"The idea here is to regard all industry, personnel, and historic beliefs as mere hypothesis, forever open to being disproven or improved upon. The trigger phrase to watch out for: 'We do it this way because that's the way it's always been done,' or, 'This is just how we do it around here.'"

2. Be Honest

"Seek out the opposing views and give them a platform. If we try and put ourselves out of business before the competition does, we'll always stay a step ahead."

3. Be Vigilant

"This simply means, we need to relentlessly seek out and root out the status quo."

"Brian, I am so impressed." Caroline glowed. "This is really insightful stuff. If you're okay with it, I'd actually like to pass this on to a few of my clients!"

"By all means!" Brian enthused. "But in the spirit of encouraging dissent, is there anything you'd add to or change here?"

Caroline nodded, thoughtful. "Not necessarily. But I do have two questions that I think would be helpful to prompt this work within your team."

1) *In what ways is our business model indistinguishable from our competition?*
2) *What aspects of our business model have remained unchanged over the past 3-5 years?*
3) *What makes us truly distinct and proud?*

Brian nodded, writing them down. "Thank you! I'll definitely use those!"

Caroline nodded. "A warning though, Brian. There are a few sacred cows in the Hierarchy, and insubordination is one of them. If this starts to catch on, be prepared to deal with some repercussions. It might spark more than you planned on!"

ULTIMATUM

As usual, Caroline's words proved true. As Brian began empowering his division from the fringes inward, giving them a voice in policy, strategy, and implementation, the ripples spread quickly. It wasn't long before he found himself in the CEO's office.

"Have you gone off the deep end?" Hank paced madly behind his desk, "You're holding open forums with rookie salespeople? Making decisions by committee?"

"Some of what we'd been doing wasn't working, so I changed it," Brian replied. "I'm doing what's best for my team and our clients in the long run. Have you ever asked why we do some of those things, or if they even still make sense today? Plus, you can't argue with the numbers. We're one of the only divisions that's actually growing. And I know my team has never been more energized and engaged."

"I can't argue with that..." Hank sat, locking eyes with Brian. "Well, the quarter's up in eight weeks. If you're not on year-end plan by then, we'll have to re-consider your new approach. We're depending on you to keep us afloat right now."

Brian blinked. "But those targets are for the end of the year, not the end of the *quarter*! You're essentially asking us to meet year-end goals a full three months early. Hank?! That's never been down before. Even if we close every deal, I don't know we have the pipeline to get there. "

Hank just shrugged, "I know, but it's the reality. Given where we're at elsewhere, it might not even..." He trailed off, clearly avoiding something. "Look, it's not a secret this is crunch time. You've got eight weeks."

Brian shook his head, unbelieving. "We're the only vertical in the company that's even managed to grow at all over the past year, and you're doubling down on only that?"

"I have to. Our projections aren't suggestions, they're promises. If we don't hit those —"

Brian's frustration erupted, "We can't let them drive us off a cliff! Chasing percentage points every three months isn't sustainable. And there will be quarters where we don't grow, that's a fact. But over the long term–"

"Brian, I don't have the long term. I have eight weeks, so that's what you have. Got it?"

Brian nodded, realizing there was no way around this. "Fine. One condition, though: total autonomy. What I'm doing is going to work, but it needs time and I don't want anyone looking over my shoulder. I get to run my team how I see fit."

Hank just shrugged, "Fine with me. Total autonomy."

Walking out of the office, Brian's mind spun. What they were being asked to do was nearly impossible. And there was something about it he didn't trust, something filling the spaces between Hank's words. Tension, frustration, and anger twisted together in his gut. He had no idea how he was going to make this happen.

That's when his phone rang.

A Way Out

"We've noticed what you've been doing at Axis, and we've heard great things around the industry. We've been looking for someone exactly like you, who knows that the rules are made to be broken and improved upon."

The voice on the other end was Melissa Gregory, CEO of Paradigm Corp., one of Axis' direct competitors."We love what you're doing there, but you have to be realistic: at a company like Axis, you're just too dynamic to last. You're an original, and Hank Stephens doesn't like originals. But we do." Her pitch went on, but the gist was simple: President of Operations, overseeing every vertical in the company. The position came with a salary bump, more autonomy, and a chance to bring the ethos that he'd begun building at Axis to a much bigger stage.

Brian knew how incredible this opportunity was. Unlike Axis, Paradigm had navigated the disruption of the past decade incredibly well, remaining notoriously flexible with their structure and methods. He tried to temper his excitement as he replied, "I'm honored, Melissa, really. Let me think about it and get back to you..." but as he hung up, he felt more conflicted than ever.

This was more than just a great promotion: *it was a way out,* free and clear. No more having to battle for every change, no more fighting the Hierarchy at every turn. But at the same time, it would mean leaving everything he'd started to build here.

Whatever he chose, he needed to do it fast.

FEAR VS. LOVE

"I don't know what I'm going to do." Brian sat across from Caroline, head in his hands. "Paradigm is a fantastic opportunity. And just when our strategies are starting to work at Axis, Hank hands me these new targets. It's like they want me to fail. And I know he isn't telling me everything."

"Do you think Axis is in trouble?"

"It's possible. Or he's setting me up for failure so he can fire me. But either way, why not just jump now? But if I leave…" He trailed off, torn.

"You're worried that you'd be giving up on everything you've been building."

"Exactly. I'd be abandoning the team. And after everything we've accomplished... would I just be taking the easy way out?" He paused, thrown. "Then again, if it's taken us this long to start turning things around, who knows how long it might take to actually start sustaining the profits we need? I'm no good to my team if I'm fired."

Caroline looked him deep in the eye. "Brian, it's time for some brutal honesty. You have to ask yourself some hard questions right now about <u>why</u> you're doing this, and you need to answer them truthfully."

"I'm doing this for the good of the team! I'm doing this because we've finally figured out who we are, and the type of culture we want to create."

"Are you sure?" Her eyes bored straight through him.

"Of course, why would you even ask that? Why else would I be doing this?"

"I ask because authenticity isn't something you do. It's something you are, something you become. Do you know why most people's attempts at authenticity fail?"

Brian was tired of Caroline's seemingly endless patience. He needed results, not more advice. He just sighed, "No, why?"

"Because what they see as genuine is actually a manipulative strategy driven by their own selfish goals, instead of a true heart posture shift that places others' needs above their own."

"You don't think I'm being genuine?" He spit back, angry.

"Only you can answer that. Do you really have their best interests at heart? Or are you just trying to accomplish the same old goals, but using a different tool to do so?" He stewed in silence, as she went on. "Growing up, we were taught that, 'he with the most toys wins.' But we all know now that the consequences of that belief are a nightmare, one that our culture is still trying to recover from. That version of the American Dream is a short-sighted race to the bottom, and the finish line is a very lonely place. Think about Ed's funeral: how many people were there because they loved him?"

"Not many." Brian's voice dropped, remembering it well. "I think most of us were there because we still feared him, even after he died…"

"I read somewhere that at most funerals, only ten people cry. I don't know about you, but I want to finish my life having touched a lot more people than that." Brian nodded, sobered. "This is the last Unwritten Rule of the Hierarchy: 'Leave your humanity at the door.' The Hierarchy teaches leaders to function transactionally, instead of transformationally. Do that for long enough, you stop seeing people as human beings."

"Look, I want all of that, I honestly do. I just..."

"You're afraid of what might happen if you truly go all in?" He looked away, knowing she was right. "Brian, I refuse to believe that the point of life is to arrive safely at death. With this much on the line, do you really want to make this choice based on fear, or do you want to make it based on love?"

He kept silent, her words detonating inside him like a depth charge. She leaned closer.

"You're either in, or you're out. *Love or fear, one or the other.* You can't half-ass this. Your team can tell if you're leading from the heart, if you actually trust them and place their own interests above yours. The Hierarchy was built on walls; between the top and the bottom, between work and humanity, between your heart and your hands. We were taught that that's what the world looks like. But it doesn't have to. You can change it. You just can't change it without going all in."

Brian nodded, and didn't say much after that. But driving home, he couldn't shake what gripped him: more than an instinct, a reality. Clear as day.

Now he knew exactly what he needed to do.

"EXACTLY WHERE YOU NEED TO BE..."

"I needed to buy a sledgehammer."

The afternoon sun was setting fast as Brian, Caroline, and Augie walked in to the dining hall after a long day in the gardens. Augie shook his head in amazement, "Brian, I've known and worked with many executives in my life, but I've never met anyone who went out and bought a sledgehammer. That's truly taking it to the next level!"

"In retrospect it seems a little dramatic," Brian admitted.

"Nonsense!" Augie insisted, "Sometimes human beings need dramatic shifts in our lives to cement the truths that we're growing into. Our spirit will prompt us to make those changes, often without us even rationally knowing why we're making them. Some people suddenly find that they need to move to a different country, change their name, or put ink on their bodies. As you said, you needed to buy a sledgehammer."

"Maybe that's true, but in the end what good did it really do? When I get home in a few days, I'll be a week behind schedule, facing the biggest test of my career, without the manpower or resources I need to accomplish it!"

"I know. Isn't that great!?" Augie laughed, loud and genuine. "You're at the edge, Brian. You have no other option but to jump. And I can see why you're afraid. But trust me, you're *exactly* where you need to be."

Brian looked at him like he'd sprouted another head. "What do you mean?"

3 Types of Transformation

"Well, let's start with your circumstances," Augie continued as they washed up, preparing for dinner. "I think you're so caught up in them, that you can't understand how irrelevant they actually are."

Brian fought the urge to yell at his new friend, "I'm probably going to lose my job! Of course I'm caught up in my circumstances!"

"I think they matter less than you realize." He read Brian's heated glance, "I'm not being flippant, Brian. I've lost my job several times as well, and in circumstances much worse than yours. It's only because I did that I know what I'm about to teach you."

Brian nodded, cooling off. "Okay. I'd love to learn, then."

"There are three types of transformation in life. They are a transformation of...

1.) Condition
2.) Circumstance
3.) Being

"Now, most people focus on the first two, condition and circumstance. If a person is cold and starving, and you give them warm clothes and food, you have transformed their condition. If a person is without a job and can't pay their bills, and you give them a high paying job, you transform their circumstances. But while these types of transformation are necessary and important, they are temporary. Unless a person experiences a transformation of being, they will likely end up in similar conditions and circumstances to those in which they started."

Brian's eyebrows rose, "What exactly do you mean by that?"

"Why is it that within five years of winning the lottery, most winners end up worse off financially than they were before winning? And why is it that over 60% of NBA players and 70% of NFL players end up broke, homeless, and divorced within a decade of retirement?" Brian shrugged, intrigued. "So many of us believe that if we could just get that job, make it to the league, hit the lottery, get that car, watch, or house, *then* everything would be different. And temporarily, yes, that is correct, but transformation of condition and circumstances are just that: temporary."

Brian nodded, musing, "Come to think of it, every time I've gotten a promotion it's a rush, but it only lasts a week or so. Then it's back to business as usual."

"That's because what we really need, but what we rarely want, is the third type of transformation: a transformation of being."

"Why wouldn't we want a transformation of being?!"

"Because of what it requires. A transformation of being is dirty, hard work. It requires deep introspection, true humility, and limitless sacrifice. It is the opposite of everything we hold dear in our society. We want insta-everything, but that's not how transformation works. It is a long, often painful process."

Brian grinned, shooting a glance to Caroline, "You mean like my last year and a half with you?" She chuckled as Augie continued…

"Yes! And that's the direct opposite of our own culture. Why eat clean and take the stairs, when you could eat a bag of chips and check on your fantasy football team instead? Why spend your time and attention reading an autobiography of someone you respect, when you could 'veg out' and catch up on the latest reality TV show? It's easier to self-medicate and self-vindicate than it is to do the hard work of risking failure to pursue your own passions or to courageously chase what sets your soul on fire."

"Both of which offer a transformation of being," Brian finished the thought.

"Exactly," Augie nodded. "Much of us get so caught up in trying to transform our condition and circumstances, that we never actually address the real issues. We need a transformation of being, and when we experience it, everything else will take care of itself. I'm sure Caroline's told you, but one of my favorite quotes is by C.S. Lewis—"

"—'When we put first things first, second things aren't suppressed, they increase.'" Brian looked at Caroline and smiled, "I know that one."

"Then you know that it's up to us to put first things first. I know your circumstances look bleak at work right now, but this week is about you experiencing a transformation of being. Let go of the your circumstances and your condition, and trust the process."

Brian shook his head. "I get what you're saying, but it just seems close to impossible."

"I know it does Brian, but you have to surrender the outcome and understand you can't control everything. The harsh reality is that you could do everything under your control and still not hit your numbers. Or you could hit your numbers and Legal could come back and tell your CEO that you have to be fired anyway. There's just all sorts of stuff outside of your control, and you are going to kill yourself and what matters most in your life if you don't relinquish control of what you can't control, and just trust the process."

"Just trust the process, huh?" Brian shook his head. "Easier said than done."

Caroline gestured to the beautiful grounds around them, "And yet, you're surrounded here by those who've learned to do so."

Augie stood, excusing himself. "I need to clean up for dinner. I'm on table-setting duty."

As he walked off, Brian shook his head, amazed. He smiled to Caroline, "I'm going to be thinking all night about what he just said. Guy sure knows his stuff."

"Yes, he does. He did write a book[1] on it, after all," she smiled.

1 *Business Secrets of the Trappist Monks,* by August Turak

"WHAT ARE YOU REALLY AFRAID OF?"

The next morning, Brian joined Augie as they performed one of the dirtiest, but most important jobs at the Abbey: spreading and bagging the mixture of compost and soil in which the mushrooms would grow. They worked in silence, until Augie asked —

"Brian, what are you really afraid of?"

Brian paused, a bit confused. "What do you mean?"

"For me, it was fear of the unknown. Even though I was President of my company, with a fantastic salary and all the perks, I knew the job was destroying me. But instead of quitting, I just held on, because I was literally more afraid of waking up on a Monday morning and not knowing what to do, than I was of giving my life to a job I hated."

"Wow! Well, I'm glad you got out," Brian replied.

"Me too. But it took years, and I'm one of the lucky ones who actually got out. When we're young, we are bold and courageous. We set out to change the world! But over time, those dreams are ground out of us. Society tells us we need to make the responsible choice, 'grow up' and get any steady job instead of doing what we love. And for a long time, I fell for that. I traded my heart for 'safety' and comfort."

"You chose a transformation of condition and circumstance, instead of a transformation of being," Brian replied.

"Yes! You've got it," Augie grinned. "But it didn't last forever. One night my wife and I were watching this stage drama, about a group of people who were trapped inside a prison for many years. Eventually, the prison doors were unlocked, and the armed guards abandoned their posts. But because of years of conditioning, the prisoners actually refused to leave. A man even came to visit them, telling them they were free to leave. But instead of listening to him, they threw him out."

Augie paused, remembering. "I knew immediately that I was one of those prisoners. I had chosen the 'comfort' of a prison, instead of true freedom. Why? Because it was easier to believe that someone else was keeping me chained up, than to accept the truth: that the only one responsible for keeping me chained up, was me."

"Wow, Augie." Brian was stunned, his mind firing. "You're not the only one. I think the same thing has happened around us."

"Of course it has! All the rules have changed, and there's no reason to stay trapped in a job you hate, but for most people in our culture, that's really hard to believe. It's hard to believe you could just walk away from prison and pursue your dreams and destiny. It's hard to believe you can stop treating people like production units and start to become a transformational leader. It's hard to believe you can shift from being a purely profit-driven organization and become a mission-driven one that operates by service and selflessness."

Brian nodded, "You bet! That's a hard one to live out in the boardroom."

"And yet the research shows time and again that purely profit-driven organizations are consistently outperformed by their mission-driven rivals. For example, look around us. The Abbey's mushroom farm is a low-margin, high-competition business. And yet, every year the demand for their product *always* outstrips supply, even at a considerably high price point for the market. They're the Nike of mushrooms! Why? Because their mission is far greater than profits. Profits don't drive their business, they simply happen as a byproduct of putting first things first."

"If that's true, why isn't the rest of the world running their businesses like the monks?!"

Augie laughed, "I ask the same thing, trust me! And I work to educate and persuade as many corporate leaders as I can of the truths I've learned here. But Brian, trust me: when you've been stuck in prison for most of your life, it's hard to believe that there are other ways of doing business. Most people will choose the three square meals per day and comfortable structure of a scheduled life, even if it is killing their potential. They prefer a comfortable nine-to-five that they can complain about, instead of embracing the pressure of accepting that anything is possible, if they commit to seeing it through. There has never been an era of greater opportunity for anyone regardless of sex, race, zip code, or last name, but like my friend James Altucher says, 'If someone insists they need to be in prison even though the door is unlocked, then I am not going to argue. They are free to stay in prison.'"

Brian sat silent for a moment, processing this. "So, are you saying I need to leave Axis?"

"Of course not! Leaving your prison doesn't always mean leaving the job itself. But it might mean doing that job in the manner you know you've been made to do it. Never forget, *ordinary life becomes extraordinary when ordinary people choose to sacrifice comfort in pursuit of what sets their soul on fire and become incredibly faithful in the little things entrusted to them.* Will you go there? It's beyond worth it. Not because of what you can achieve, but because of who you can become in the process.

And the place to start is knowing what it is you're truly afraid of. So, I'll ask again: what are you really afraid of?"

Brian paused. Even after their discussion, he didn't have an answer. "I… I honestly don't know."

"Whatever it is, Brian, it will surface before you leave. And I'll warn you, you may not like what it is. But in order to become the leader you were meant to be, you must overcome it, no matter what. Breaking through my own fear of the unknown was the best decision of my life, and it set me free to a life I've never once regretted."

The Purpose Driven Lie

"Have you ever heard of the purpose-driven lie?" Augie and Brian were returning from a lunchtime walk along the river. Brian shook his head, "No, but I'm excited to hear about it!"

"So, like anyone who's worked in corporate America, I'm sure you probably have a thing or two to say about corporate mission statements."

"Like the fact that they're mostly hot air?" Brian chuckled.

"You said it!" Augie laughed. "Here's the thing: mission statements aren't inherently bad. They're actually great. But the reason we all have that reaction, is because of the irony we've all lived through of hearing those lofty, aspirational words said in meetings, but living out a day-to-day reality at the company that's often the exact opposite!" Brian chuckled, remembering Axis's mission statement, as Augie continued. "The reality is that most people in the business world are chasing their own goals instead of actually letting a mission guide their choices. Often, those who claim to be leading a purpose-driven organization are really using those stated ideals to cloak their own selfish motives."

Brian nodded, "As opposed to actually doing what you say you're going to do."

"Correct. In a word, that's authenticity. It's easy to see when an organization doesn't have it, too: just watch what they do when the pressure is on and actually living out their mission will cost them something. It's easy for the NBA to take a stand against discrimination and human rights violations by pulling the All Star game from North Carolina, but they're noticeably quiet when it comes to being in business with China, whose list of human rights violations is longer than an extra innings baseball game."

"More often than not, 'mission statements' are usually just more marketing."

"Yes! And individuals live like this as well. One of my mentors founded IBM's Executive School, and he would run a fascinating exercise where the participants were given a case study about an IBM employee who, despite faithful service to the company for twenty years, had struggled recently with no signs of improvement. Half the participants were told that IBM was losing serious money that year, and the other half were told the opposite."

Brian began to shake his head, "I think I can see where this is going."

"The half who were told IBM was in the black always argued passionately for keeping the employee, and the group who saw a different financial report argued just as passionately that he should be fired. And while at first their arguments centered on morality and ethics, sooner or later it always came down to what really mattered: money. The exercise revealed the true motives behind their decision-making processes."

Brian nodded, "I know exactly what you mean. But how do I change? How do I authentically live a mission driven life?"

Augie looked at him with compassion, "I can't tell you the answer for you Brian, but I can tell you what the Trappist monks do here. Their mission is to serve God and serve others. Therefore, it often doesn't matter what they are 'doing' at any given time, because what they're really doing is serving God and serving others. Ironically though, this detachment is what makes their businesses do so well and allows them to make 'tough' decisions very clearly. They are never over-invested in anything they're doing. They're able to simultaneously care more by caring less."

Brian nodded, watching a line of monks walk back to the sheds after noon prayers. Augie continued, "Now, their business does very well, but it's not from focusing on making a profit and hitting goals, it's from persistently pursuing a lofty mission. The truth is, most people don't have the courage to live that out, and the sad thing is that they miss out on some pretty incredible things because of it."

THE DREAM

Augie's words stayed with Brian as he went back to work that afternoon. In fact, for the rest of the day, he couldn't stop thinking about his career and role at Axis. Had he deluded himself into believing that he was putting first things first, when he was really still just focused on hitting a bottom line? Had he truly been pursuing Caroline's lessons for the benefit of his team and his mission, or was it all really just about getting an 'edge' that would benefit himself in the long run?

Even as he drifted off to sleep, his mind was still turning. What seemed like a moment later, he blinked awake, noticing the familiar smell in the room: Pall Malls. "Wake up, son." Brian shot up, startled, because sitting in a wooden chair nearby was —

— Ray, sawdust on his Levi's, smoking. Brian rubbed his eyes. "You're wondering if this is a dream, aren't you son?" Brian nodded. "Well, if it is or if it isn't, does it matter?" Brian shook his head, stunned silent. "Anything you want to say?"

Of course, there were a thousand things, but what came out of Brian's mouth first surprised him. "I'm sorry I wasn't there when..." A long pause. "There was a big account I had to close in Maryland that week, and... I was working."

"Well, you learned from the best, didn't you? Following the recipe for success, just like your old man."

Brian shook his head, adamant, "I'm not like you. I'm changing things."

"I can see that. You still sure they're not working you too hard at that desk?" Brian's chest tightened, filling with the familiar surge of desire to prove himself. Ray just kept smoking. "What kind of weeks you putting in lately?"

"I'm not falling for that."

"Falling for what? It's a simple question. Are you workin' hard, or hardly workin'?" Ray nodded at Brian's silence. "Yeah, that's what I—"

"I'm working the hardest I've ever worked, doing the most important work I've ever done, okay?! I'm putting in as many hours as it takes!"

"To do what?"

"To hit my numbers and save my job, that's what!" Brian shot back, reflexive.

Ray chuckled. "Well, then. Guess we're not so different after all."

The moment those words hit Brian, he knew Ray was right. Even after all of his training and transformation, a shred of him was still a pure 'results guy,' just like his father. Somewhere deep down, he was still holding onto the goal of hitting the numbers. He hung his head, as Ray stubbed out his cigarette on the arm of the chair. "Well, time for me to be on my way. Got a tee time at nine. Finally have time for it now."

"Hey, Dad…" Brian paused, "What was it like, after you got the diagnosis? What did it feel like to know that you were dying?"

Ray shrugged, "What does it feel like to pretend that you're not?" He said as he stood, and walked out, letting the door close with a —

— SLAM! Brian's eyes snapped open as he surged up in bed, wide awake, every nerve firing. He gasped a few deep breaths, trying to calm himself, realizing that what he'd just experienced was only a dream. But dream or not, there was no shaking the overwhelming power of the experience.

SURRENDER

The next day was Brian's last at the Abbey, and he spent most of it in silence, thinking about the night before. Late in the day, he and Caroline found themselves alone at the edge of the property, overlooking the river as the sky above exploded with color. While Brian hadn't shared his dream yet, Caroline seemed to sense his unease. "Long night?"

Brian let out a long sigh. "You have no idea."

She nodded, as if she very much did have an idea. "Well, maybe this can help. I was prompted to share something with you that I learned in my desert years. In Japan, I had the honor of meeting an old samurai archer named Akira, who said one of the wisest things I've ever heard. He told me...

'The ultimate illusion of the human experience is control. The person you want beside you in battle is the man who has surrendered the outcome, and surrendered to the fact that he might die. When you surrender the outcome, you are freed up to be at your best, to be in the moment, and to trust your training. It is the one who has surrendered the outcome who ironically has the greatest chance of survival. It is the one who has surrendered the outcome who has the greatest chance of success. It is the one who has surrendered to the fact that he could fail, who has the greatest likelihood of not failing. Until you surrender the outcome, you will always be the greatest enemy to your own success. In order to reach your greatest potential you must operate with a heart posture of gratitude, commit to the controllables, surrender the outcome, and trust the process.'[2]

2 Excerpt from, Chop Wood Carry Water, by Joshua Medcalf

"Now, surrendering the outcome doesn't mean you care less, or don't give your very best. It just means that you let go of what's outside your control. Many mornings I surrender things that I desperately want to control, but know I don't have control over. Surrendering the outcome is about having peace about that which is outside of our control, without sacrificing the effort or care of what is inside of our control."

Brian nodded, letting those words sink into him. Caroline shifted, "I'm sure you're wondering about where to go from here, about what will happen once you're back at Axis on Monday. But I think it might be helpful to take Akira's words to heart and think about what you need to surrender. Ask yourself, what have you been trying to control that is outside of your control?"

"The results," Brian answered instantly, overcome by emotion. The words poured out of him, their raw energy unleashing a weight that he'd felt for decades. "I need to surrender the results. I need to surrender keeping my job, hitting the new numbers, and being the perfect leader for the team."

A long pause, as Caroline smiled. "That's been a long time coming, hasn't it?"

Brian laughed, feeling lighter already somehow. "Again, you have no idea!"

"I worked next to you for twenty years, Kelly, I do have some idea!" she replied. "I always knew you were a 'results guy,' but I always hoped that one day you might learn a different way to do things."

"And I have," Brian nodded, sobered. "This past week here, it's been… pretty remarkable. I'm excited to take what I've learned and activate it at work."

"I know you will," Caroline smiled. "I'm so proud of you, Brian. You've come a long way. No matter what happens with Axis, I know you're going to be okay."

Brian tried to keep the anxiety out of his voice. "I hope you're right."

Caroline just hugged him, and turned toward the Abbey. "Come on, we don't want to miss dinner. I heard Augie made his famous spaghetti sauce!" Brian just laughed and followed her in, overcome by the beauty of the past week, and overcome with gratitude for the lessons he'd learned and the kindness he had experienced.

Back to Reality

On Monday, Brian gathered his team. Recharged by the past week, he was more focused and present than he'd ever been, but he knew the task they faced would take everything he'd just learned, and more. His eyes burned with resolve as he scanned their faces.

"I have something to admit to all of you. We've spent the past two years trying to dismantle element so the Hierarchy that no longer serve us in this division, and I've been so focused on that task that I missed the problem at the heart of all of it: me. Yes, the system is flawed, but people like me perpetuate it. Even after all we've been through, I've still put the results before living out our mission, and that stops today."

He gathered himself. "Frankly, I don't care if we hit Hank's numbers. I don't care if I lose my job. That doesn't mean I won't give everything I have to try to push this across the line, but at the end of the day it's not what matters. What matters is all of you, and the work we're doing here to add value to our clients and the world around us."

A voice rose from the team, "But do you really think we can pull this off?"

"Honestly, I don't know. What I do know is that we've spent the last two years preparing to be the type of team that's capable of pulling this off. You're equipped, and you're empowered. If anyone can do this, it's us. Now, let's trust that training, focus on what we can control each day, and release what we can't." Heads nodded around the room, as he continued, "What we're going to do isn't going to be easy, or safe. But a very wise friend told me recently, 'I refuse to believe that the purpose of life is to arrive safely at death.' I know I haven't always modeled that ethos well, but I believe it with my whole heart. So I'm jumping into this and wagering my entire career on all of you. No pressure."

He paused, a few chuckles rippled through the anxiety as the room shifted. Instead of being intimidated, the team seemed enlivened. Brian grinned, "Let's go make it happen gang." As they scattered, buzzing, his mind was already speeding to his first appointment. He wasn't excited about it, but he knew it had to be done.

The Gloves are Off

Lunch the follow day would prove to be a very important moment for Brian and Axis. As he checked his watch and scanned the bar, Brian thought to himself, "*Is he going to show up?*" Then...
"Brian?" He turned to find a familiar face — Austin. Brian couldn't help but notice that he had the same rushed, paper-thin look that Brian himself had worn for years. But Austin couldn't hide his surprise, as he gave Brian a once-over. "Almost didn't recognize you. Have you been working out or something?"

"Something like that. How are you?"

Austin deflected, "Grinding away, you know the drill." He ordered a double, wasting no time. "So, why are you here? You need a killer idea to steal and take credit for?"

"Austin, I'm so sorry. The last time I saw you wasn't one of my best days. I'm here to apologize, first and foremost. But I can promise you that a lot has changed."

"Has it?" Austin gave him a cynical grin.

"I promise you, it has. The gloves are off." As Brian unfolded his story, he could see Austin's facade crumble. Brian finished off from the heart: "I was operating under a lot of Unwritten Rules of the Hierarchy at the time, and I treated you terribly as a leader and a boss by stealing your idea and taking credit for it publicly. And despite the fact that it's unforgivable, I really hope you can forgive me, because I really care about you as a leader, as a man, and as a friend."

Austin was silent, inscrutable. Then, "I appreciate that, honestly. And here's the thing," he admitted, "It wasn't just you. I was wrong, too. Not that you weren't, because taking credit for your employee's idea is pretty low. But you weren't wrong about me. I wasn't really ready for a promotion."

"Really?"

"Of course! Look, it was only after I got to Sartis that I started to understand what you were teaching me. You were trying to make me better, and I didn't get it." A brokenness laced his words, the perspective of maturity. "As soon as I stepped into a bigger role, I made some costly mistakes, got into situations that I just didn't know how to handle. I'm better for that, but it was painful and I couldn't help thinking, 'Damn it, Brian was right. If I only knew then what I know now...'"

Brian laughed, "We can all be shortsighted."

Austin just shook his head, taking it in stride. "I should have heard you out."

"So why don't you hear me now?" asked Brian. He leaned in, passionate. "Come back to Axis. If I've learned anything from the past few years, it's that life's too short to waste doing work you hate for people who don't challenge, empower, and inspire you to do your best. And on my side, we really could use you. You already know the ins and outs of the division from a product and client side. Of course, we do things a little differently these days, but something tells me you can keep up."

"How 'different'?"

"You'll see. But if you jump in, I can promise I'll help you fill in some of those knowledge gaps, and together we can make the division better than it's ever been. What do you say?" Brian watched as Austin traced the condensation around his glass, silent.

Finally, he raised it and drained the drink, smiling. "All right, boss. When do we start?"

Leaving it All on the Field

The next seven weeks blurred past, and the change in the air was palpable. Brian's team was engaged, energized, and inspired, and with Austin jumping right back in, they were practically unstoppable. They attacked each day's list of controllables, checked them off, and then processed their performance as a team each night. By the time Brian dismissed the team at the end of Week Eight, he smiled with pride as he saw the final sales figures: *they more than doubled the projections.*

So on Monday morning, he was surprised to find Hank more rumpled than normal, his office a war zone of empty takeout containers and dirty cups. He glanced around the messy office, concerned, "Everything okay?"

"Yeah, of course! Just a few late nights." Hank swiped a stack of papers earmarked with red 'Sign Here' tabs from his desk, holding up Brian's Sales Report. "You know, I wish every one of my SVP's was as good as you. You and the team really nailed this."

Brian exhaled, relieved. "Glad to hear it!"

"Whatever you're doing, keep doing it. You guys are all safe, and you will be for as long as I'm here." Brian nodded, his smile growing. "Now, go spread the good news. I'd do it myself, but I've got another meeting here in a minute."

Brian thanked him, rushing down to his floor to spread the good news. As the team exploded with relieved cheers, Austin wrapping him in a grateful hug, and Brian enjoyed every second, knowing the value of days like this.

Their hard work had paid off, and he'd lived to fight another day at Axis.

"WHAT COMES NEXT?"

But the next morning, the air of energy, excitement, and positive expectation was gone. Instead, Brian was greeted by a funereal silence, people passing by in hushed whispers. It didn't take long to figure out why.

A knot of his team members clustered around a TV watching CNBC, tight-faced with anxiety. The bottom runner read, "AXIS FALLS TO MORE HEALTHCARE DISRUPTION" as the host intoned, "*–CEO Hank Stephens announced today that Axis will be sold within the next two weeks, prompting a sharp uptick in the stocks of rivals–*"

Brian wavered on his feet, stunned. *How could he be so stupid?* The last seven weeks, it had been a suicide mission, probably to give a few bottom lines an uptick and improving the selling price. He bit back a surge of fury, fighting to contain himself.

"Why didn't you tell me?!" Ten minutes later, Brian paced an empty hallway.

"Honestly, it wouldn't have mattered," Hank's voice crackled through his phone. "I know Ortho is the only vertical that's worth anything, but it just wasn't enough to keep the whole ship afloat."

"So who's buying us?"

"Renovatio, some hedge fund out of San Jose. They've been doing a lot of this I guess, scooping up the struggling med tech companies over the past couple years."

"So we'll be auctioned off?" Brian deflated. He'd heard the horror stories about funds like that, who moved in like vultures and scrapped struggling companies for parts.

"Don't worry, your desk will be empty long before then. Executive level is always the first to go," Hank laughed. "At least you get that killer severance package, right?"

Brian didn't laugh back. "What the hell am I supposed to tell my team?"

"Nothing. Everything. At this point, it doesn't really matter, does it?" Hank hung up, leaving Brian alone in the silent hallway. He sighed, feeling the helpless weight of it all.

When he told the team, their outrage was exactly what he expected, and he didn't blame them. He just held up a hand for quiet. "Look gang, I'm sure I'll be the first to be let go, but I want you all to know I'm just proud of what we accomplished. Axis or not, no one can take that away from us..."

He scanned the room, emotion rising as he realized what he saw staring back at him in every face: gratitude. He swallowed the lump in his throat, knowing that he was far from a man who deserved that. Overwhelmed, he thanked them all collectively, before individually speaking with as many as he could, until only he and Austin remained.

Austin spoke first. "For the record, you're the best boss I've ever had."

"Austin, I'm basically the only boss you've ever had."

"Oh, I know," Austin laughed. "Still, I'd be lucky to work for someone like you again."

"And I'd be lucky to ever work *with* someone like you again." They shared a smile, looking out over the quiet Orthopedics floor. The momentum that filled it over the past few months had vanished, along with all the possibilities Brian hoped would open up.

"So... what do we do now?"

Brian just blinked as it hit him: "Honestly? I don't know."

Judgement Day

The next day found Brian sitting alone outside the Boardroom. Each Axis executive was meeting with Renovatio's management individually, and he knew what that likely meant. So far, not a single executive had been kept on.

Intent on shifting his focus, Brian pulled an Axis brochure from a nearby stack, noticing an old marketing image featuring the once-familiar Mission Statement: 'Healing the world through innovation, progress, and connection.' Brian chuckled, *I wish Caroline were here.* They'd been through so much together here, and despite how things were ending at Axis, he had an incredible journey to be thankful for.

He dialed her number, and as the call went to voicemail, he couldn't help leaving her a message. "Hey, so I'm about to face the firing squad here. And it's actually a lot more bittersweet than I thought it would be. I'm really going to miss this place. I'll find something else I'm sure, but my heart was here, with my team." He trailed off, resisting the temptation to stew in regret. "It's too bad, that's all. "

Memories came hard and fast as he continued, "I just wanted to thank you for helping me find my life again. Whatever happens from here on, I know I'll have the tools to face it, because those are all tools that you gave me. Well, except for the sledgehammer." He chuckled, "Thank you, Caroline. Thank you for being an amazing friend and a patient teacher. Even though my time here is ending, at least I've been able to make the most of it, thanks to you."

As he hung up, a secretary motioned to the Boardroom. *Your turn.* He stood, each step bringing him closer to the end. But as he entered the room, two things struck him...

First, the Boardroom was empty, except for one person.

Second, that person was Caroline.

The Long Game

"Caroline? What are you doing here? I'm supposed to be meeting with my new bosses."

"You are." Brian's mind ground to a screeching halt, as Caroline's eyes twinkled.

"Wait, what? Are you a part of Renovatio?"

"The founder and CEO, yes."

"So this is your job? It has been this entire time?"

"I do 'a little consulting,' yes." She gave him a knowing grin. "It started small, but I quickly realized there needed to be a bigger piece to it. So with the help of a few clients, I started Renovatio about five years ago."

"But isn't this fund a vulture? You gut struggling companies and sell them for parts–"

"Do you know what 'Renovatio' means, Brian? It means 'to renew.' We exist to save companies who have lost their heart, or who are too bought into the Hierarchy to evolve and survive. Of course, we save what can be saved, but it's all with the mission of eventually shepherding them back into the new world of work."

"You're playing the long game?" She nodded as Brian began to realize, "So this whole time, you helping me out with everything at Axis, that's what this has been about...?"

"Not always. But as I saw how fully you committed to what we were learning... well, you've never been afraid to be the last one on the court. Your division really has you to thank for their success, because you cared enough to never give up."

"Well, I have you to thank for that!" They shared a smile. Then, Brian's expression clouded, "So, why are we here? Am I being let go?"

Something in Caroline's eyes told him she'd been looking forward to this moment for a very long time. "Brian, we're here because of your *heart.* As long as I've known you, it's been your greatest asset. And all these years, I knew if I could access your heart, you'd become the leader I've always known you could be. More than just a savvy businessman: a transformational leader who leads from the heart and empowers talented workers to do their best work toward a single transformational mission."

She continued, "Over the past two years, that's exactly what's happened. Not only did you turn your division around, you did it in a way that has inspired and transformed the lives of your employees. After the news went out that we were buying Axis, do you know how many emails, calls, and letters Renovatio received on your behalf? We received one from every single person who works for you. *Every. Single. One.*"

Emotion caught in Brian's chest, as she went on, "Axis isn't dead, it just needs some rebuilding. It's going to be a long journey and a difficult job, but someone has to do it. And I want that someone to be you."

Brian glowed, hopeful. "Really?"

"I wouldn't want anyone else. We can get into the specifics, but starting today, if you accept, you're acting President and CEO of the new Axis Medical."

For a moment, speech failed him. Brian's head seemed to wobble, truly overwhelmed by the offer. It felt like an eleventh-hour pardon to a death-row inmate, a chance to live again after he was certain everything was ending. But not just survive. To live and work to his fullest potential.

"Brian? What do you say?"

He just looked up, smiling wide, answering the only way he knew how… "You're on."

THE FIRST DAY OF THE REST OF YOUR LIFE, PT. 2

These days, Brian's 'alarm clock' looked a bit different. Morning light splashed the walls of his home office, as the sound of birds drifted through his half-open window. He took in the morning's beauty with a sense of overwhelming gratitude, and a steady furnace of genuine excitement at the limitless potential standing before him. He enjoyed the sounds and sights of the morning for a bit before he focused himself, undertaking what had been his morning routine for almost a year now: his gratefulness mediation and 5 Minute Journal.

As he pulled into the parking lot at Axis's new location, he couldn't help but remember his first day on the job, over twenty years ago. Sure, he wore jeans and a button-down now, but today wasn't all that different. He felt the same anticipation, the same promise that the horizon was his for the taking. The horizon was just a lot bigger today.

Energy began to hum through the building as employees trickled in, laughter and excitement flowing as the workday took its first few steps. Brian entered his office, a glass-walled room at the center of it all. And that's when he noticed it: a small gift box sitting on his desk. Curious, he slid the card open, recognizing Caroline's handwriting instantly. It said simply…

"Never forget how you got here. xo, Caroline."

Brian grinned, pulling off the paper. He opened the box, and his face lit up as he saw her gift. Inside, modeled to desk-sized scale in cast iron, was a single item...

A sledgehammer.

The End.

Contact Info: Seth Mattison

Website: www.sethmattison.com / www.justluminate.com
Facebook: https://www.facebook.com/sethmattison
Twitter: @sethmattison
Instagram: @sethmattison

Cell: 612-269-9219
Email: sethmattison@gmail.com

Keynote Speaking: www.sethmattison.com

Leading Breakthrough Performance Workshops in Collaboration with Ryan Estis: www.estismattison.com

LUMINATE COMMUNITY: This is the best way for us to stay connected while we work to provide consistent value to your life as we address the big issues impacting the way we work, lead, live, and love in this new digitally charged world. At justluminate.com you will gain access to our community of influences and luminaries, articles, videos, podcasts, courses, assessments, mp3's, and other tools as they're rolled out. We can't wait to connect with you. Join at www.justluminate.com

Thank You's From Seth

Frist and foremost I'm grateful for my remarkable wife Kristen. You were there in the very beginning. In the small rooms and the little stages. Always supporting whether it was emotionally, financially, or simply holding down the home front while I traveled endlessly learning my craft and collecting these stories, you are always there supporting this dream. Thank you. I love you.

Thank you to Joshua for pushing me to write this book and then agreeing to collaborate on it with me. If it wasn't for you brother, this book would not be. You inspire me every day.

Thank you to my parents Brad and Joliene Mattison for giving me the foundation on which to build this business and my life. I am who I am because you are who you are. I couldn't have asked for a better environment to grow up and learn the most important lessons in life. You're both remarkable leaders that pour into people at every chance you get.

Thank you David Stillman and Lynne Lancaster. You believed in me when all I had was potential. You saw something in me and then graciously and generously poured into me. Your coaching and mentorship was and continues to be, second to none. My ability to connect with an audience from stage today can be traced back to watching the two of you masterfully do it for years. Thank you for believing in me. Thank you for giving me a shot. Which all any of us can ask for. Thank you both for guidance when it came to telling this story. Lynne – Thank you for always pushing me to go deeper and look harder for truth. To always fight to be fair and balanced in our approach and to know the value of where we've been while simultaneously creating the future.

I'm incredibly grateful for my dear friend and collaborator Ryan Estis. There is not a day that goes by that I don't give thanks that you're on this journey with me. You're like the brother I never had. I wouldn't have been able to level up from where I was without you're wisdom, knowledge, and perspective. You push me every day to get better. To have started in this crazy business at virtually the exact same time and to grow together has been one of the greatest blessings in my life and I couldn't be more excited about the future. Cheers to big big things to come brother.

Thank you Jacob Roman for helping us tell a story that we believe mattered and needed to be told. You were right there with us every step of the way. I could always feel your passion, energy, and enthusiasm for what we were trying to do. You're a workhorse and craftsmen of the highest order.

Thank you to all of my clients over the past decade and all of the individuals that have shared your stories of transformation with me. I carry all of you with me as I move forward on my own journey of transformation as a storyteller and someone trying to leave a mark on this world.

Contact Info: Joshua Medcalf

Twitter: @joshuamedcalf
Instagram: @realjoshuamedcalf
Cell: 918-361-8611
Email: Joshua@traintobeclutch.com

Keynote Speaking- t2bc.com/joshua

Mentorship Program- Our mentorship program isn't a good fit for everyone, but we are always willing to see if it is a good fit for you. It is a serious investment of time and resources. Email Joshua@traintobeclutch.com for more information.

T2BC Reading Challenge- People are consistently telling us how going through our reading challenge has radically improved their business, family, and personal life. It is available to download under the *free stuff* tab at t2bc.com

The Experience- *Transformational Leadership Retreats.* We bring together people from all over the country to engage in a day of interactive learning. We also create space for fun activities like golf, surfing, or snowboarding with the t2bc team.

The Clutch Lab- Our T2BC podcast takes a deeper dive into leadership, life-skills, and mental training.

T2BC 101 Online Video Course- With over 20 short video sessions, you can use this course individually or to teach your team the T2BC curriculum. It is a great next step tool. Available at **t2bc.com/training**

Join the T2BC community- This is the best way for us to provide consistent value to your life and for us to develop a long term relationship. You will get articles, mp3's, videos, and other tools as they come out. It's also free. ☺ Join at t2bc.com

Books- You can always order signed copies of any of our books by emailing us, and they are also available on iBooks, Kindle, Amazon, and through our publisher.

The first book we wrote is, ***Burn Your Goals.***
The second book we wrote is, ***Transformational Leadership.***
The third book I wrote in conjunction with this book is, ***Hustle***
The fourth book I wrote is, ***Chop Wood Carry Water***
The fifth book I wrote in the same vein as this one is, ***Pound The Stone.***

YouTube- Our channel is *train2bclutch*

Thank You's From Joshua

I'm incredibly grateful to my mother, who has supported me and been one of my best friends my whole life. Thank you for never giving up on me when no one would have blamed you if you had.

Thank you to my father, who did the best he could with what he had.

Thank you Seth for being an incredible friend, mentor, and allowing me to be apart of this project and helping to tell a story that needed to be told.

Thank you Judah Smith for being the most amazing pastor a person could ask for. You have taught me so much about Jesus, and how He really feels about me. I don't think anyone has ever had such a profound impact on my life in such a short period of time as you have.

I'm so grateful to Jamie and Amy, you both have been such an amazing support system in my life, and I'm so grateful I get to spend so much time with you. Thank you for creating a safe space for me to be me devoid of judgment.

Thank you Lisa for always being there to hear my articles, or just to listen to another one of my crazy stories, and for being an incredible best friend!

Thank you Russ and Skip for all the mentorship over the years. Thank you Skip for being one of the first people outside of my family to financially invest in me and my dreams.

Thank you Andy and Terry for teaching me so much as a teenager. I wouldn't be here today without your love and wisdom.

Thank you Jacob Roman for helping us create work that we are really proud of, and for your dedication to your craft. You are a true craftsman!

Thank you to all the people who have given me the great privilege and responsibility of mentoring you and speaking into the lives of those you lead. I have learned so much, and I am truly grateful for the opportunity to work with you.

Thank you Jesus for your extravagant, reckless, relentless, and undeserved love.

CPSIA information can be obtained
at www.ICGtesting.com
Printed in the USA
LVOW12s1516110418
573087LV00001B/37/P

9 780692 827574